W9-CAD-392

LOVE
WALKED
AMONG
US

LOVE WALKED AMONG US

LEARNING TO LOVE LIKE JESUS

PAUL E. MILLER

NAVPRESS

Discipleship Inside Out™

Discipleship Inside Out™

NavPress is the publishing ministry of The Navigators, an international Christian organization and leader in personal spiritual development. NavPress is committed to helping people grow spiritually and enjoy lives of meaning and hope through personal and group resources that are biblically rooted, culturally relevant, and highly practical.

**For a free catalog go to www.NavPress.com
or call 1.800.366.7788 in the United States or 1.800.839.4769 in Canada.**

Library of Congress Catalog Card Number: 2001032605

ISBN 978-1-57683-240-0

Cover design by Jennifer Mahalik
Cover background art by PhotoDisc
Creative Team: Don Simpson, Liz Heaney, Darla Hightower, Glynese Northam

Some of the anecdotal illustrations in this book are true to life and are included with the permission of the persons involved. All other illustrations are composites of real situations, and any resemblance to people living or dead is coincidental.

Unless otherwise identified, all Scripture quotations in this publication are taken from the Holy Bible: New International Version® (NIV®). Copyright © 1973, 1978, 1984 by International Bible Society. Used by permission of Zondervan Publishing House. All rights reserved.

Miller, Paul E.
    Love walked among us : learning to love like Jesus / Paul Miller.
        p. cm.
    Includes bibliographical references.
    ISBN 1-57683-240-6
    1. Love--Religious aspects--Christianity. I. Title.
    BV4639 .M49 2001
    241'.677--dc21   2001032605

or Jill

Contents

ACKNOWLEDGMENTS

My wife, Jill, more than anyone, made this book possible by pointing me to Jesus. I am also indebted to Ron McRae and Anita Mathias for teaching me to write. Liz Heaney continued to teach me while she edited the book and made it readable. I've also benefited from the editing of my coworker, Keith Howland, and the wisdom of my good friend, David Powlison. I am thankful as well for all those who read and reflected on the manuscript. And lastly, I am grateful to Bob Allums for believing in this book when it wasn't much more than an idea.

WHO IS JESUS?

N 1991 MY WIFE, JILL, ASKED ME, "DO YOU LOVE ME?" We had been going through a hard time, but hard times weren't unknown to us. We have six children whose ages at the time were 2, 5, 8, 12, 14, and 16. Our eight-year-old, Kim, is disabled—unable to speak, unable to do many things other children do. Sometimes Jill got so tired that she'd fall asleep during dinner.

It had been a long day, and I thought she just wanted me to reassure her that I loved her. "Of course I love you," I said. But then she asked me again, "Paul, do you love me?" The third time she asked, I got irritated with her. Of course I loved her. Didn't I help out with the kids? In the morning I dressed the little guys and got them breakfast. In the evening I read to them and put them all to bed. I helped constantly. Case closed. That night I went to sleep fuming at Jill, still making a list of all the ways I loved her.

I didn't tell Jill, but her question gnawed at me. What does it mean to love someone? What does love look like?

As I thought about love, I began to think about Jesus. After all, Jesus is supposed to be the most merciful and self-giving person who ever lived. I decided to study his life to see how he related to others. What was he like? How did he treat people?

And slowly by slowly, as they say in Africa, I began to understand what it really means to love.

Who Is Jesus?

Regardless of your background, Jesus is hard to ignore. Almost two billion Christians claim to follow him; more than one billion Muslims honor him as a prophet. Leading Jewish theologians esteem him as a great rabbi. His image can be found in Hindu temples. Many cult leaders claim to be a reincarnation of the spirit of Jesus.

Jaroslav Pelikan, professor emeritus of history at Yale University writes:

> Regardless of what anyone may personally think or believe about him, Jesus of Nazareth has been the dominant figure in the history of Western culture for almost twenty centuries. . . . It is from his birth that most of the human race dates its calendars; it is by his name that millions curse and in his name that millions pray.[1]

Despite all the attention Jesus gets, most people have little idea of who he is as a person, even those who worship him. I have often asked Christians, "When you get to heaven, what person in the Bible would you like to meet?" Only one out of several hundred has mentioned Jesus. I think the word "person" throws them off because they aren't used to thinking of Jesus as a person.

When we see Jesus portrayed, he often comes across strangely. Hollywood frequently pictures Jesus in slow motion. In most films Jesus talks slowly, walks slowly, and moves slowly. He also stares. My ten-year-old daughter, Emily, and I were watching one of the better Jesus films, and we noticed that he never blinked! The other actors did, but Jesus never did. Our

16

eyes began to hurt every time the camera focused on Jesus' face.

I decided to study Jesus with fresh eyes, forgetting what I already knew—or thought I knew—about him. I wanted to experience what Albert Einstein did when he read the Gospels. He reflected:

> I am a Jew, but I am enthralled by the luminous figure of the Nazarene. . . . Jesus is too colossal for the pen of phrase-mongers, however artful. . . . No man can read the Gospels without feeling the actual presence of Jesus. His personality pulsates in every word.[2]

Einstein was not a follower of Christ but he felt the wonder of the real man in a way many miss. As I read and studied the Gospels, I began to experience Einstein's sense of wonder. I hope you do too.

WHAT ARE THE GOSPELS?

Matthew, Mark, Luke, and John, the Bible's four accounts of Jesus' life, are called *gospels*, a word that means *good news*. They each carry the name of the author, and were written over 1,900 years ago in Greek, the language of the Roman Empire. Like modern biographers, each author provides his own unique perspective and includes scenes or details that other authors don't. When we put their accounts together, we get a rich, three-dimensional picture of Jesus. Like documentary videos, scenes are often described in such vivid detail that we can visualize exactly what's happening: the setting, the circumstances, the people, and how Jesus treated them.

Matthew, a former tax collector and one of the original twelve followers of Jesus, wrote an eyewitness account. Tax collectors in the Roman Empire were usually well educated and fluent in both their native language and Greek. The government auctioned off the job of tax collector to the highest bidder. The winner of the auction recouped his expenses by charging more than was required, thereby alienating the general population. Think of Matthew as a very smart, former used-car salesman. Though he's been changed by Jesus, he could still read people like a book. There are hints of this in the details Matthew provides about Judas (the disciple who betrayed Jesus).

Written about thirty-five years after the death and resurrection of Jesus, Mark's account was most likely derived from Peter, a former fisherman and the leader of the twelve disciples. Like Peter's personality, Mark's story is fast-paced and passionate, and it captures the shocking impact Jesus had on people.

Luke, a doctor and a traveling companion of Paul (one of the leaders in the early church), based his chronicle on the testimony of eyewitnesses. His book breathes compassion for the "little" people and the powerless: outcasts, women, children, the poor, and the disabled.

John, another former fisherman and one of Jesus' most intimate friends, wrote his gospel last. As someone particularly close to Jesus, John gives us unique, close-up glimpses of him.

Are the Gospels reliable history? I'll let you judge for yourself. My only request is that you read them with an open mind, the way Einstein did. Einstein reflected about the Gospels,

> No myth is filled with such life. How different, for instance, is the impression which we receive from an account of the legendary heroes of antiquity like Theseus! Theseus and other heroes of his type lack the authentic vitality of Jesus.[3]

C. S. Lewis, Oxford professor and a leading expert on myth, wrote:

I am perfectly convinced that whatever else the Gospels are, they are not legends. I have read a great deal of legend and I am quite clear that they are not the same sort of thing. They are not artistic enough to be legends.[4]

When we read a myth or legend, we instinctively understand that we are in the world of fable. We switch gears when we read it; in the words of the poet Coleridge, we "suspend disbelief." But the Gospels are set in a real world of needs: wine running out at a wedding; hungry crowds with not enough food; fruitless fishing trips; and no money for the tax bill. Into this world quietly breaks the miraculous, which seems as ordinary as the hassles. In myth, extraordinary people in an extraordinary world do extraordinary things. In the Gospels, the extraordinary love and compassion of a remarkable man radiates and illuminates an ordinary world.

A Study of Love

This book examines how Jesus treated the people he encountered, because it's in "little moments" with friends and family that most of us reveal our true selves. Jesus is no exception.

Gandhi, a Hindu and national leader of India, enjoyed chiding Christians that they did not take seriously Jesus' call to love. Yet, what is more difficult to learn than love? How do you love someone when you get no love in return—only withdrawal or ingratitude? How do you love without being trapped or used by the other person? How do you love when you have your own problems? When do you take care of yourself? How do you love with both compassion and honesty? When you are compassionate, people use you; but when you are honest, people get angry. What is love?

Most of us have lacked good models for love. We don't even know what's normal anymore. Let me suggest this: The person of Jesus is a plumb line to which we may align our lives. He

19

satisfies our hunger for a hero—someone who is both good and strong—to change this world.

Jesus arrived at the home of his good friends, Mary and Martha, several days after their brother Lazarus died. Mary, in the passionate way of the ancient Near East, threw herself weeping at Jesus' feet. Overcome with grief, Jesus weeps with her. Several bystanders comment, *"See how he loved him!"* (*John 11:36*). In this book we'll join the bystanders of Jesus, look at Jesus, and *see how he loved.*

PART 1
LOVE
SHOWS
COMPASSION

CHAPTER ONE

A MIND FULL OF SOMEONE ELSE

LOVE LOOKS AND ACTS

*J*ESUS LIVED 2,000 YEARS AGO IN A TIME VERY DIFFERENT from our own. His world was almost entirely Jewish; only an occasional Gentile appears in the Gospels. His was a world of close-knit families—individuals didn't exist apart from their extended families. All a person had was family and clan. If you lost them, you lost everything.

When Jesus is about thirty he gathers a group of disciples and begins walking from town to town throughout Israel, teaching people. One day while approaching the city of Nain, Jesus and the disciples encounter a funeral procession. Luke records what happened:

> *Soon afterward, Jesus went to a town called Nain, and his disciples and a large crowd went along with him. As he approached the town gate, a dead person was being carried out—the only son of his mother, and she was a widow. And a large crowd from the town was with her. When the Lord saw her, his heart went out to her and he said, "Don't cry."*
>
> *Then he went up and touched the coffin, and those carrying it*

stood still. He said, "Young man, I say to you, get up!" The dead man sat up and began to talk, and Jesus gave him back to his mother.

They were all filled with awe and praised God. "A great prophet has appeared among us," they said. "God has come to help his people." This news about Jesus spread throughout Judea and the surrounding country. (Luke 7:11-17)

Nain is nestled in a beautiful valley in southern Galilee where the Jewish tribe of Issachar had settled. The Old Testament tells us that the land is pleasant (Genesis 49:15). Nain sounds like pleasant in Hebrew, but for this mother the day was anything but pleasant.

Her son — her only son — has died. And this is not the first time she has had to bury a loved one. She is a widow. The greatest joy for a Jewish woman was to bear a son; to lose a son, the greatest sorrow. The loss of her husband and only son means a life of poverty. With them she has lost the equivalent of her pension, Social Security, and Medicare. Guilt is likely compounding her despair, as the premature death of a child was believed to be the punishment for sin.[1] Possibly the town gossips were wagging their heads, wondering what she did to deserve losing everything.

Jewish funerals were usually held at six in the evening, after the day's work was done. Earlier in the day she'd laid her son's body on the floor of her home, groomed his hair, dressed him in the best clothes she could find, then placed his body on an open wicker basket, face up, arms folded. The town had gathered at her door to help bury her son. The women lead the procession because the Jews believed that a woman's sin brought death into the world, so women should lead it out — adding shame to sorrow. As the funeral procession winds through the streets, many symbolically share the mother's burden by taking their turn holding the basket. Paid mourners and flute players follow in the rear, chanting, "Weep with them, all you who are bitter of heart." Most of the five

LOVE WALKED AMONG US

hundred or so people from Nain would have come because this loss was so significant.[2]

Map of Northern Palestine

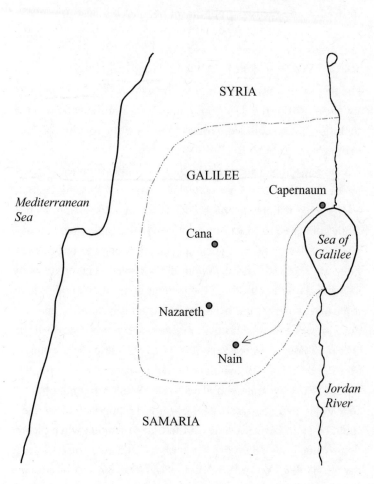

SYRIA

GALILEE

Capernaum

Mediterranean Sea

Cana

Sea of Galilee

Nazareth

Nain

Jordan River

SAMARIA

The graveyard is to the east of the city, along the road that winds its way down to Capernaum, Jesus' home base. The Greek text suggests that the crowd with Jesus is larger than the crowd coming out of Nain—probably more than a thousand people are with Jesus. Jesus arrives just as the funeral emerges from the gates of the city, and the two groups meet.

He Feels What She Feels

The first thing Jesus does is look at the woman. *The Lord saw her*— not the crowd or the dead son. Jesus singles out the widow in the confusion of two colliding crowds. And when he sees her, *his heart went out to her (Luke 7:13).*

Compassion is the emotion most frequently attributed to Jesus. How can you tell that a person feels compassion? What did people see on Jesus' features in this scene? After all, compassion is quite subtle compared to anger or fear. When I ask people what compassion looks like, they say it's communicated through a person's eyes: They are soft and tender, attentive, concerned. The entire body pauses and listens, absorbing the feelings of another. Perhaps Jesus stops mid-sentence and becomes quiet, transfixed, as he looks at the widow. Or maybe his eyes moisten, and a tear rolls down his cheek. Whatever his reaction, it is noticeable despite the commotion and distraction of hundreds of milling people.

Jesus sees a woman who is half-dead. While we think of death and life as two separate categories, the Hebrews thought there could be an in-between state. In the Old Testament when Naomi returns home after burying her husband and two sons, she tells the town folk: *"Don't call me Naomi [means pleasant]. . . . Call me Mara [means bitter], because the Almighty has made my life very bitter"* (Ruth 1:20). Naomi was alive, but she felt dead. The widow, like Naomi, has entered a living death, cut off from life, from hope.

Jesus knows this, and he experiences her pain: *His heart went out*

LOVE WALKED AMONG US

to her. Literally he was moved with compassion. Jesus enters this woman's world, feeling what it's like to be in her place.

HE BRINGS HOPE

"Don't cry," Jesus tells her. He feels her anguish, but he is not lost in it. He feels what she feels, yet is separate from her.

Someone might say that Jesus has interrupted her grieving process. Today's psychology tells us not to tell someone how to feel. But when my daughter scrapes her knee and comes in crying as if she is about to die, I tell her, "Don't cry; it will be okay" — because it really *is* going to be okay. And Jesus knows this woman has reason to hope and not weep.

Respect for the dead led to a right-of-way in traffic, so Jesus' crowd has likely divided and pulled off to the sides to let the widow and her dead son pass. At this point Jesus stops the funeral by quietly touching the coffin. Most men would stop a large crowd by shouting or waving their arms. People with less power tend to overstate it, like a teenager who slams the door because of a parental curfew. But people with real power tend to understate it, like a Caesar who decides life or death with only the slight gesture of a thumb. His action has the subtle majesty of an ancient king. What Jesus does next is pure, raw power for good. He says, *"Young man, I say to you, get up!"* The once-dead, young man obeys Jesus, sits up, and starts talking.

The crowd is *filled with awe and praised God. "A great prophet has appeared among us,"* they said. After four hundred years of silence, a prophet had come. Less than three miles away and eight hundred years before, the prophet Elisha had raised an only son to life. Elisha had gone through many gyrations in his miracle, but Jesus effortlessly raised the widow's son to life. Someone greater than Elisha is here.

Word about Jesus spreads far and wide. People are reminded of God's power, and they worship him because of what they saw

Jesus do. They sense they are no longer alone with their problems, because God is visiting them in Jesus.

He Never Loses Sight of Her

With the addition of the funeral procession, the size of the crowd has nearly doubled. Every eye is on Jesus. Nothing like this has happened before. It's even unusual for Jesus—only two other times does he do a miracle like this. The miracle is rife with possibilities—book deals, movie rights, and talk show appearances!

But Jesus' eye is on the widow. He takes her son by the hand, helps him off the basket, and walks him over to his mother. He's not thinking about himself and how he can benefit from this amazing display of power. He isn't distracted by his own miracle—he remembers the person. He cares for both the son's physical need and the mother's emotional need.

Jesus possesses both tenderness and power. Usually tender people lack strength and strong people lack gentleness. But Jesus shows both goodness and strength.

Not Efficient

Charles Spurgeon was a famous preacher in London more than one hundred years ago. Though a caring husband and a gentle man, like all of us, he was flawed. His wife, Susie, once told about a time when she went with her husband to a large auditorium where he was to speak:

> We went together in a cab, and I well remember trying to keep close by his side as we mingled with the mass of people thronging up the staircase. But by the time we had reached the landing, he had forgotten my existence; the burden of the message was upon him, and he turned into

the small side door where the officials were awaiting him, without for a moment realizing that I was left to struggle as best I could with the rough throng around me.[3]

Sound familiar? A large crowd, a frightened woman, and a religious teacher. Except here the teacher forgets the woman because he is thinking about what he wants to say. Jesus forgoes a sermon for the sake of a person. But Spurgeon ignored a person for the sake of a sermon. It got worse:

> At first, I was utterly bewildered, and then . . . I was angry. I at once returned home, and told my grief to my gentle mother. She wisely reasoned that my husband was no ordinary man, that his whole life was dedicated to God and that I must never, never hinder him.

Then Spurgeon returned home, upset that he couldn't find his wife:

> My dear mother went to him and told him all the truth. Quietly he let me tell him how indignant I had felt, and then he repeated mother's little lesson pointing out that before all things, he was God's servant.[4]

Did you notice how God got dragged in? Somehow God was the reason Spurgeon ignored his wife. So his wife gets lectured by both her mother and her husband for feeling hurt. God isn't revealed in Spurgeon's life through this incident; he's the excuse for not loving.

Spurgeon and I have a lot in common. When Jill shared her heart—both good and bad—I would "fix" her. One time when she was agonizing over Kim, I told her, "Why don't you just give her to God?" Her reply shut me up: "I do. I do every day."

Other times I was unaware of what Jill was feeling. I didn't realize what having a disabled child had done to her friendships, her future, and her dreams. Even though I did things for her, I began to understand why Jill wondered if I loved her. I realized that I was good at "raising the dead son," but I didn't take time to look, to feel, and to walk with Jill. I was already looking for the next "dead son." When I focused on the task and not Jill, she felt the difference. Jesus' tenderness suggested to me a new, less "efficient," way of relating.

Love, I realized, is not efficient.

When the Exxon *Valdez* spilled thousands of gallons of crude oil along Alaska's shoreline, the company's president dismissed the suggestion that he go and see the damage—implying that a trip would be a waste of his time. He had the power, but he lacked goodness. What might it have done to his heart to have gotten down in the muck and cleaned a few geese?

Jesus has shown us how to love: Look, feel, and then help. If we help someone but don't take the time to look at the person and feel what he or she is feeling, our love is cold. And if we look and feel, but don't do what we can to help, our love is cheap. Love does both.

Chapter Two

LOOKING SHAPES THE HEART

LEARNING HOW TO SEE PEOPLE

HEN I COME HOME FROM WORK, SOMETIMES I GO through the mail while listening to Jill tell me about her day. I sound something like this: "Uh-huh, yes Jill, that's interesting, uh-huh." When I do this, Jill gets irritated because I've made her feel that the mail is more important to me than she is. When she talks to me, she wants my attention, and she knows she has it when I look at her.

As I studied how Jesus loved, I was surprised by the number of times that Jesus looks at people. Altogether the Gospels mention Jesus looking at people about forty times. I was particularly struck by how often his compassion for people was preceded by his looking. Here is just a sampling:

> When he saw the crowds, he had compassion on them, because they were harassed and helpless, like sheep without a shepherd. (Matthew 9:36)

Jesus looked at him and loved him. (Mark 10:21)

*When Jesus saw his mother there, and the disciple whom he loved
standing nearby, [he asks his closest friend, John, to take care of his
mother]. (John 19:26-27)*

Jesus Models Looking and Teaches Us How to Look

Jesus describes the same pattern in his parables. (Parables are simple stories that are meant to change how the listener thinks. Like Jesus' behavior, they are often startling.)

The parable about the Good Samaritan tells how a Samaritan rescues a man who is mugged and beaten by robbers on the Jericho–Jerusalem road, a notoriously dangerous stretch of highway. To understand how this story must have shocked the Jews, imagine someone telling a story about "The Good Nazi." The Jews and Samaritans hated one another.

In the parable two religious professionals (a Levite and a priest) pass by the man in the ditch, fearful of involvement. Then a Samaritan stops, bandages the man, takes him to an inn, and pays the bill. Jesus' description of how the Samaritan cares for the wounded man is identical to how he himself approaches people: *"But a Samaritan, as he traveled, came where the man was; and when he saw him, he took pity on him. He went to him and bandaged his wounds, pouring on oil and wine" (Luke 10:33-34).* The Samaritan sees, has compassion, and acts.

The Samaritan sees a person. The priest and the Levite see a problem. They are too distracted, preoccupied, or agenda-driven to identify with him. Maybe they had neither the time nor the energy to be bothered by someone's troubles.

In the parable about the Lost Son the younger of two sons demands his inheritance while his father is still alive—in effect, wishing his father were dead.[1] He then leaves home and spends

LOVE WALKED AMONG US

all his money on wild living. Finally, starving and homeless, he decides to return to his father and beg for forgiveness. *"But while he was still a long way off, his father saw him and was filled with compassion for him; he ran to his son, threw his arms around him and kissed him"* (Luke 15:20). To spot his son *a long way off* this father had to be scanning the horizon, putting all his energy into looking—especially since he didn't know when (or if) the son would come home.

When we confront a new or difficult situation, we can become confused or overwhelmed. Often we don't even know how to begin. But we can look. We might not feel compassion, but we can concentrate on the other person. By keeping the other person in front of us, we are opening the door to compassion.

When talking about people who had opposed building a leper colony, Mother Teresa said, "Once they saw, they understood."[2]

Love begins with looking.

Looking Is Risky

Why are so many of us like the priest and the Levite? Why do we look away from hurting people? We have many reasons. The hassle. The dirt. The risk. The cost. The commitment.

When Jesus touched the casket of the widow's son, he became ritually unclean. Touching the dead defiled him. When the father welcomed his lost son, he faced not only the shame of looking ridiculous but also—as we shall see in the next chapter—the anger and rejection of the "good" son who stayed home. If the beaten man was dead, the priest and the Levite risked being ritually unclean for two weeks. Best to keep moving...?

But the Samaritan interrupted his schedule and emptied his moneybag. Because he is an outsider, he ran the risk of the wounded man's family seeking him out for vengeance when he took him to an inn. One scholar said this about the risk the Samaritan took: "An American cultural equivalent would be a Plains Indian in 1875

33

walking into Dodge City with a scalped cowboy on his horse, checking into a room over the local saloon, and staying the night to take care of him."[3]

We instinctively know that love leads to commitment, so we look away when we see a beggar. We might have to pay if we look too closely and care too deeply. Loving means losing control of our schedule, our money, and our time. When we love we cease to be the master and become a servant.

Jesus is not just offering good advice. He tells this parable to disrupt our "safe" world so that we can begin to see people and stop looking through the narrow lens of "our group." Unless we do that, we won't be able to love.

A Move Outside of Self

When I was studying how Jesus looked at people, I watched how Jill looked at Kim. Kim is bright and cheerful, but struggles getting around physically and has trouble communicating because she cannot speak. She has few friends. The local public school where she attends has several floors with steep steps and difficult railings. Jill had memorized Kim's schedule and prayed for her during the hard parts of the day. When Kim was navigating the steps, Jill was praying for her safety. When Kim was alone in the lunchroom eating, Jill was thinking about her. With her heart full of Kim, she quietly concentrated on her and then prayed for her all day. She was "looking" at and looking out for Kim even when she wasn't with her. When Jill looked, she slowed down and concentrated. She moved outside of her world and into Kim's.

When I think of how Jesus loved people, the word "cherish" comes to mind. When we cherish someone, we combine looking and compassion—we notice and care for that person. We don't shut him or her out. We cherish things that make us feel good and are valuable to us: jobs, approval, investments, cars, or sex. But we

34

tend not to cherish people — even those closest to us. A magazine writer describes this scene:

> Last summer, on as lovely an evening as one can hope for in central Virginia, I was at my daughter's lacrosse practice. Standing next to me was a father more intent on the cell-phone conversation he was having (which did not sound terribly pressing) than on watching his daughter play. Time and again, she would look toward him craving his attention, but he never saw her. Nor, for that matter, did another girl's mother see her child, focused as she was on her laptop, merrily tapping away.[4]

Both of these parents struggled to cherish their child. Cherishing is the beating heart of love. It means that during the day your eyes are on others. All of us long to be cherished, yet we are often slow to cherish others. We want someone else's mind to be full of us, for someone to care about how we're doing each moment of the day.

When I've messed up — been harsh or impatient — with Jill or one of our kids, I've usually failed in some way to see them, to notice them. I'm focused on my agenda, my thoughts, and my feelings rather than on the other person. To be lovers of people, we need to look at them. Like Jesus we must see them. Like him we must stop, look, and listen.

LOOKING SHAPES THE HEART

Jesus points out how looking can change us when he cautions against loving money: *"For where your treasure is, there your heart will be also. The eye is the lamp of the body"* (Matthew 6:21-22). A heart that focuses on money will eventually be shaped by money. We begin to resemble what we focus on. If we devote our lives to our jobs, then we mentally take the office to our daughter's lacrosse game.

35

Perhaps this is why Jesus warns us so vehemently about misusing our eyes. When talking about the danger of sexual lust, he exaggerates for the sake of emphasis, *"If your right eye causes you to sin, gouge it out and throw it away"* (*Matthew 5:29*). In other words, how can we even think of using our eyes—which are meant to fill our hearts with love—for degrading people into sex objects?

If the eye is the lamp of the soul, then the soul of Jesus is filled with people.

THE EYES OF LOVE

Corrie ten Boom was a Dutch woman whose family hid Jewish people in their home during World War II. Corrie, her sister, and their father were caught and imprisoned by the Nazis for this. Her father died in prison, and her sister died in a concentration camp. Corrie survived to tell this story from her childhood:

> A person who influenced my life in my late teens was a man from India. As a boy he had come to hate Jesus. He knew about God, but the Bible of the Christians was a book which he believed was a gigantic lie. Once he took a Bible and burned it, feeling that with this act, he could publicly declare his scorn of what he believed were the untruths it contained. When missionaries passed him he threw mud on them.
>
> But there was a terrible unrest inside of him; he longed to know God. He told this story about himself:
>
> "Although I had believed that I had done a very good deed by burning the Bible, I felt unhappy. After three days, I couldn't bear it any longer. I rose early in the morning and prayed that if God really existed, He would reveal himself to me. I wanted to know if there was an existence after death, if there was a heaven. The only way I could know it

for sure was to die. So I decided to die.

"I planned to throw myself in front of the train which passed by our house. Then suddenly something unusual happened. The room was filled with a beautiful glow and I saw a man. I thought it might be Buddha, or some other holy man. Then I heard a voice.

"'How long will you deny me? I died for you; I have given my life for you.'

"Then I saw his hands—the pierced hands of Jesus Christ. This was the Christ I had imagined as a great man who once lived in Palestine, but who died and disappeared. And yet now stood before me . . . alive! I saw his face looking at me with love.

"Three days before, I had burned the Bible, and yet he was not angry. I was suddenly changed . . . I saw him as Christ, the living One, the Savior of the world. I fell on my knees and knew a wonderful peace, which I had never found anywhere before. That was the happiness I had been seeking for such a long time."

That weekend as I listened to the Sadhu, I was amazed but disturbed. He told of the visions he had seen—of how he really saw Jesus—at a time when he didn't believe.

One boy ventured to ask the question we all wanted to know. "Please, sir, how did Jesus look?"

He put his hands before his eyes and said, "Oh, his eyes, his eyes . . . they are so beautiful." Since then I have longed to see Jesus' eyes.[5]

A friend of mine went through a very hard time in her life. She told me that in the middle of the night, she woke up to a vision of two eyes looking at her. I asked her what they looked like. She said they were brimming over with tears, and that they were Jesus' eyes. It gave her the courage to hang in there through some trying times.

LOOKING SHAPES THE HEART

I don't know how much stock to put in visions, but I was struck that both of these visions centered on Jesus' looking at people with love. If we know we are loved—that someone is looking at us—then we can give love; then we can look at others.

The Gospels suggest that when we watch Jesus, we are watching God love us. Like the father in the parable about the Lost Son, God is waiting, looking, his eyes glued to the horizon searching for us. When he sees us, even though he is a dignified patriarch, he lifts up his garment and shamelessly gallops toward us, as we come trudging toward him with our load of guilt and despair. He wraps us in his arms and smothers us with kisses.

This is not new behavior for God. He has looked at people with compassion for centuries. When the Israelites were enslaved, God said, *"I have indeed seen the misery of my people in Egypt . . . and I am concerned about their suffering"* (*Exodus* 3:7). Jesus' eyes give God a face.

LOVE WALKED AMONG US

CHAPTER THREE

"I KNOW WHAT'S BEST FOR YOU"

JUDGING BLOCKS COMPASSION

E HAVE A FRIEND WHO USES A WHEELCHAIR DUE TO the weakening effects of muscular dystrophy. One day he was at a restaurant with a group of friends. When it was his turn to order, the server turned to his friends and said, "What does he want?" Her thinking was simple: "People in wheelchairs are not normal. You can't talk to odd people. So I'll talk to his friends." He had ceased to be a person and had become a mere object, an extension of his wheelchair. The server put our friend—an electrical engineer—into a category, instead of seeing him as a person.

Treating people like objects comes easily. I was sweeping the kitchen floor, and Jill was at the counter washing dishes. When I got to where she was standing, I tapped her ankle with the broom so that I could sweep the floor under her. She never said anything; she just quietly moved out of the way. Only then did I realize what I had done. We tap objects to move them, but we speak to people—especially our spouses!

A Problem or a Person?

In the first century disabled people had to fend for themselves by begging along the side of the road, usually by the gates of the city so people couldn't avoid seeing them. Few cared for the weak. The heroes were powerful, healthy people, like Alexander the Great, who forced their will on others.

But Jesus is different.

> *As he went along, he saw a man blind from birth. His disciples asked him, "Rabbi, who sinned, this man or his parents, that he was born blind?"*
>
> *"Neither this man nor his parents sinned," said Jesus, "but this happened so that the work of God might be displayed in his life. As long as it is day, we must do the work of him who sent me. Night is coming, when no one can work. While I am in the world, I am the light of the world."*
>
> *Having said this, he spit on the ground, made some mud with the saliva, and put it on the man's eyes. "Go," he told him, "wash in the pool of Siloam" (this word means Sent). So the man went and washed, and came home seeing. (John 9:1-7)*

Jesus silently looks at the man, perhaps showing the disciples how to love by deliberately pausing. He focuses his attention long enough for the disciples to begin a discussion about the man. They ask Jesus, *"Who sinned?"* They automatically judge the man for his blindness. In their first-century cultural grid, either he or his parents messed up. They just need Jesus' help to categorize him. But Jesus cuts through their judging by telling them the blind man doesn't fit into either of their boxes.

It is no longer fashionable to talk about "sin," but we've not lost our ability to be judgmental. Our knowledge of psychology has increased our ability to see people or their actions as wrong, bad, inferior, messed-up, or dysfunctional. In other words, we see "sins"!

We analyze one another all the time: "Did he have a troubled childhood, or is he just naturally that way?" We get a little insight into a person, put him in a box, and conclude, "He should really be in therapy" or "He has issues."

Analyzing provides the disciples with a safe and tidy world that keeps everything in its place. So they talk about the blind man while they are right in front of him. But Jesus moves toward him, makes mud, and touches his eyes. Jesus lowers himself in order to care, while the disciples elevate themselves in order to judge.

The disciples see a blind man; Jesus sees a man who happens to be blind. The disciples see an item for debate; Jesus sees a person, a human being like himself. They see sin, the effect of man's work; Jesus sees need, the potential for God's work. The disciples see a completed tragedy and wonder who the villain was; Jesus sees a story half-told, with the best yet to come.

It is one thing to notice a blind man; it is quite another to stop and talk with him—that gets scary. He might ask for money or interrupt our schedule. It's as if we are afraid that his blindness might affect us. This fear is not irrational—when we pause to have compassion, something of the other person's problems comes on us. Some of his pain touches us. At the very least, slowing down and noticing someone takes time.

Compassion affects us. Maybe that's why we judge so quickly—it keeps us from being infected by other people's problems. Passing judgment is just so efficient.

If I had been compassionate with the blind man, I would likely have judged the disciples for being callous, and then given myself a pat on the back. The satisfaction I'd feel in observing the disciples' insensitivity would have buoyed my spirit, but Jesus is tender with them. He doesn't rebuke or shame them—he simply answers their question.

How do you think the blind man felt if he heard the disciples' question? I suspect he felt put down and pigeonholed—possibly guilty or angry. Maybe he wondered: "What did I do to deserve this blindness? Was it my parents' fault? Was it me?" He might have judged them back: "those idiots. . . ." Even if their comment made him angry, I imagine that he was left with an uneasy, hopeless feeling: "What did I ever do. . . ?"

In the first century people saw suffering and wondered what the person did to offend God. The sufferer directed his anger at himself. In the twenty-first century we respond by being offended at God. The sufferer gets angry at God. How surprised the blind man must have been to hear Jesus' reply to the disciples' question: *"Neither this man nor his parents sinned, but this happened so that the work of God might be displayed in his life."* Instead of condemning him, Jesus called his blindness an opportunity for God to work in his life. The man's darkness is a door to God's light. <u>Through suffering we will see God</u>. Jesus takes something that appears to be ugly and broken and begins to make it beautiful and whole, even before he heals the man's eyes.

Jill and I have seen God begin to do that with us.

When Jill was pregnant with Kim, she thought of the Old Testament psalm that says, *The LORD will keep you from all harm* (121:7). But then God gave us a "harmed" daughter. We didn't understand why. Thinking about that promise made Jill feel even worse. It hurt to hope.

When God gave us Kim, he gave us something we loved very much but couldn't control. She constantly drained our reserves. Jill and I are naturally quick, confident—and judgmental. Once, before Kim was born, Jill was washing the car in our driveway and our neighbor passed on the sidewalk. A young mother herself, she said to Jill, "I don't know how you have the strength to do everything that you do." Jill replied, "If you're organized, you can get a lot done. You should try it." Years ago, I was in downtown

Philadelphia with a friend, and a street person passed us. He slurred out something incomprehensible to me, and I dismissed him. As we were walking away my friend asked me, "Why did you talk to him like that? He just wanted to know where the soup kitchen was."

I smile at the work of God displayed in our lives, at God's sense of humor. Jill and I have spent countless hours with Kim doing speech therapy, helping her articulate her slurred words. I've spent hundreds of hours programming Kim's speech computer, which she is very proficient at. Jill no longer has time to be organized. When I ask her where some money has gone, she smiles at me and tells me that she doesn't know. She has sworn off being organized. She just can't do it anymore.

God gave us Kim to keep us *from all harm*—to keep us from being so self-righteous and "together." God used Kim to bring us to the end of ourselves, to teach us about love, and to teach us about himself. Our lives no longer worked—we had to learn how to live from the bottom up. Like the blind man, we found glory in a most unexpected place.

The Blind Man Comes to Life

As the story of the blind man unfolds, the politically correct "morals police" of the day, the Pharisees, get wind of the healing and bring in the former blind man for interrogation. They're upset that Jesus worked on the Sabbath by restoring the man's sight. Like all good bureaucrats, they miss the obvious and focus on what they see as an error. Sabbath observance was the most visible sign that one was a Jew. So by violating the Sabbath, Jesus has trampled on a symbol of national identity.

The blind man proves to be an astute observer. He's the smartest of the bunch. After an initial interrogation, the Pharisees interview him again, seeking to find fault with Jesus. They're in a quandary. On the one hand, Jesus keeps doing amazing miracles that would seem to point to God as the source. But on the other hand, he keeps irritating them by breaking their religious rules.

> *A second time they summoned the man who had been blind. "Give glory to God," they said. "We know this man [Jesus] is a sinner."*
>
> *He replied, "Whether he is a sinner or not, I don't know. One thing I do know. I was blind but now I see!"*
>
> *Then they asked him, "What did he do to you? How did he open your eyes?"*
>
> *He answered, "I have told you already and you did not listen. Why do you want to hear it again? Do you want to become his disciples, too?"*
>
> *Then they hurled insults at him and said, "You are this fellow's disciple! We are disciples of Moses! We know that God spoke to Moses, but as for this fellow, we don't even know where he comes from." (John 9:24-29)*

Under a veneer of politeness, the Pharisees ask the man-who-can-now-see open-ended questions. They want him to join them in judging Jesus. Knowing full well that they really despise Jesus, he asks them—with a show of innocence—if they want him to repeat his story because they secretly desire to become disciples themselves! His ironic, taunting question strips away all pretense of an even-handed evaluation. He is not only perceptive and bold, but he has a sense of humor as well![1]

Failing to get what they want from him, the Pharisees lash out at both him and Jesus. Their last comment, *"we don't even know where he comes from,"* is possibly an allusion to Mary being unmarried when Jesus was conceived. If so, they are calling Jesus a bastard.

But the former blind man is quick on his feet. Years at the bottom of the heap of humanity have enabled him to see clearly.

LOVE WALKED AMONG US

The man answered, "Now that is remarkable! You don't know where he comes from, yet he opened my eyes. We know that God does not listen to sinners. He listens to the godly man who does his will. Nobody has ever heard of opening the eyes of a man born blind. If this man were not from God, he could do nothing."

To this they replied, "You were steeped in sin at birth; how dare you lecture us!" (John 9:30-34)

His response enrages the increasingly sightless Pharisees. How can someone *steeped in sin from birth* teach us — we who are so good, so educated, and so powerful? Ironically, the Pharisees answer the disciples' first question, *"Who sinned?"* The blind man did. Exasperated, they throw him out of the synagogue — a first-century shunning that would ostracize him socially. No big deal; he's already spent his whole life on the street. His friends are bums and beggars. It's as if the Pharisees have fired someone who isn't their employee.

Jesus gets wind of what happened and searches for the man. The first time they had met, Jesus looked at him, and the man was able to see with his eyes. This time he is able to see with his heart. First outer healing, then inner healing.

Jesus heard that they had thrown him out, and when he found him, he said, "Do you believe in the Son of Man?"

"Who is he, sir?" the man asked. "Tell me so that I may believe in him."

Jesus said, "You have now seen him; in fact, he is the one speaking with you."

Then the man said, "Lord, I believe," and he worshiped.

Jesus said, "For judgment I have come into this world, so that the blind will see and those who see will become blind."
(John 9:35-39)

Jesus completes the healing by connecting with the person. This is a shocking connection for a first-century Jew who only worshiped God. By accepting worship, Jesus tacitly claims to be divine, to have the authority to judge. Jesus concludes by judging the judges, the blind who think they see.

The Secret of Compassion

Jesus said that his primary way of relating to people is saving them, not evaluating them: *"For I did not come to judge the world, but to save it"* (*John 12:47*). That not only describes his whole life, but the individual moments of his life, like this brief encounter with the blind man. I'm slowly learning what this means for my own brief encounters.

It was a typical morning at our house—eight people using one bathroom, gulping down breakfast, making seven lunches, everyone rushing out to three different buses, kids whining and complaining—in short, absolutely crazy. This particular morning Jill had had it and was letting everyone know it.

My initial response would have been to give her advice, but by watching Jesus I was beginning to see that my quickness to correct people was a form of judging. So I slowed down and entered Jill's world by asking her to tell me what she was feeling. She vented for almost an hour. By the end, I realized how frustrated she was with the lack of help from our older kids. Once I understood what the real problem was, I knew how to help her.

That evening I sat down with the older kids, explained Mom's frustration, divided up the chores with them, posted a list of jobs on the side of the fridge, and told the kids I was now the family bad guy if the jobs weren't done. I had taken Jill's frustration on myself. Love often doesn't erase worries—it just shifts them to a different set of shoulders—our own.

A few months later, Courtney, our oldest daughter who was

seventeen at the time, came home late one night after being out with her friends. She came in the back door and was immediately angry with me because I was going to make her do her job — sweep the kitchen floor. I hadn't even said anything to her, but since she knew it was her chore, she just started complaining. I was tempted to remind her that with a large family we all have jobs to do; everyone in a community has to work. You know — your typical, knee-jerk parental lecture.

But since I'd been thinking about my tendency to judge I kept my mouth shut and asked if she wanted to talk about it. She didn't. Then I asked if I could help her sweep — she said "no." Finally, figuring I had nothing to lose, I said, "Courtney, sit down." She did, and I asked her what was going on. She poured out a story of how a friend of hers had put her down and had judged her for something. As we talked Courtney relaxed and all the anger drained away. When she finished, I helped her sweep the floor. If I'd followed my initial reaction and just analyzed Courtney, I would have missed out on an opportunity to love my daughter and see the world through her eyes.

Judging is knee-jerk, quick, and bereft of thought, while compassion is slow and thought-filled. By slowing down so that I could feel compassion, I was closer to both Courtney and Jill. If I'd speeded up and judged, I would have been distant from them. Judging separates and, thus, destroys community; compassion unites and creates community.

Henri Nouwen, a Catholic priest who left a teaching position at Harvard to care for disabled adults, wrote:

> In order to be of service to others we have to die to them; that is, we have to give up measuring our meaning and value with the yardstick of others. To die to our neighbors means to stop judging them, to stop evaluating them, and thus to become free to be compassionate. Compassion can

never coexist with judgment because judgment creates the distance, the distinction, which prevents us from really being with the other. . . . *"Do not judge and you will not be judged yourselves"* is a word of Jesus that is indeed very hard to live up to. But it contains the secret of a compassionate ministry.[2]

We'll often notice things wrong with people, but does that initial look lead to compassion and helping, or to judging and distance? Compassion and judging are two different ways of "seeing." When we stop judging, we rest from the incessant work of analyzing others. We don't need to figure out what's wrong with people—that's God's job. Our job is to try to understand.

two ways to see
judging eyes — God's job
compassionate eyes — our job → understand people

Self-righteousness = BAD BREATH (Halitosis)
↓
others smell it... you don't!

CHAPTER FOUR

"I'M BETTER THAN YOU"

SELF-RIGHTEOUSNESS BLOCKS COMPASSION

A BAD HAIR DAY IS JUST THAT: A BAD HAIR DAY. Everyone sees it, including you. But bad breath is different. Others smell it, but you can't. Self-righteousness—thinking that we are better than someone else—is like bad breath. Others can smell it, but you can't.

We see this in the parable about the Lost Son. Although the father is ecstatic that his son has come home, his older brother is livid when he hears that his father is throwing his brother a party:

> *"The older brother became angry and refused to go in. So his father went out and pleaded with him. But he answered his father, 'Look! All these years I've been slaving for you and never disobeyed your orders. Yet you never gave me even a young goat so I could celebrate with my friends. But when this son of yours who has squandered your property with the prostitutes comes home, you kill the fattened calf for him!'" (Luke 15:28-30)*

Good
guy
but...
✱

Compared to his brother, the older son is truly a good guy, but all he can see are his own accomplishments. Because he looks at his own goodness, he can't look at his brother as his father does. His "goodness" (freezes) him, making him (incapable) of moving toward his younger brother. Like judging, self-righteousness prevents compassion.

judging / self-righteousness prevent compassion.

A STUDY OF SELF-RIGHTEOUSNESS

Throughout the Gospels, Jesus comes down hard on people who are self-righteous, especially the Pharisees.

> *Now one of the Pharisees invited Jesus to have dinner with him, so he went to the Pharisee's house and reclined at the table. When a woman who had lived a sinful life in that town learned that Jesus was eating at the Pharisee's house, she brought an alabaster jar of perfume, and as she stood behind him at his feet weeping, she began to wet his feet with her tears. Then she wiped them with her hair, kissed them and poured perfume on them.*
>
> *When the Pharisee who had invited him saw this, he said to himself, "If this man were a prophet, he would know who is touching him and what kind of woman she is — that she is a sinner."*
> (Luke 7:36-39)

Jesus was a well-known rabbi, so news of an invitation to a Pharisee's house would have traveled around town. Likely all the people in this story had heard Jesus teach in the synagogue.[1]

At banquets Jews adopted the Greek custom of lying on a couch, facing the table with their feet extended out. In addition, the host ensured that his guests' feet were washed, as they would be dirty from walking on dirt roads in open sandals. But in this incident a woman *who had lived a sinful life* washes Jesus' feet.

When Simon sees her, he "assumes" that Jesus has failed to read

LOVE WALKED AMONG US

this woman correctly. Appearance was all-important to the Pharisees, and Jesus' complete lack of concern for appearance shocks Simon. But Simon wants to appear good, so rather than confronting Jesus openly, *he said to himself . . . that she is a sinner.* The word "sinner" suggests that the woman has either been condemned by the synagogue for adultery or is a known prostitute. Simon concludes that Jesus is not a prophet but a phony, because he sees so poorly. But Jesus not only sees the woman as she really is; he also sees Simon as he really is. ⬅

To give Simon some credit, Jesus' behavior is startling. Think about it. Imagine that you are a guy, lying on a couch, and an attractive woman enters the room and begins to cry at your feet. She lets down her long hair (which, in Simon's culture, was done only in the presence of her husband) and drapes it over your feet to wipe her tears. As she does this, she covers your feet with kisses. Finally, she takes the small jar of perfume she carries around her neck and pours it over your feet. Every eye is on you. Your feet are being touched and kissed by a well-known prostitute. Are you feeling uncomfortable? The scene is very intimate and personal—and public! Most ⊗ men in a similar situation—in any culture—would be embarrassed.

But Jesus seems unconcerned about anyone's reaction. He not only permits the woman to touch him, he also appears to enjoy her attention. Sensing his heart of love, she weeps at his feet. Her heart is broken by her sin—all her previous ways of getting love seem so empty compared with this man, this merciful and gracious lover of people.

Jesus turns his attention to Simon:

> *Jesus answered him, "Simon, I have something to tell you."*
> *"Tell me, teacher," he said.*
> *"Two men owed money to a certain moneylender. One owed him five hundred denarii, [a denarius is a day's wage for a laborer] and the other fifty. Neither of them had the money to pay him back, so he canceled the debts of both. Now which of them will love him more?"*

Pride is as ugly as prostitution!

Simon replied, "I suppose the one who had the bigger debt canceled."

"You have judged correctly," Jesus said.

Then he turned toward the woman and said to Simon, "Do you see this woman? I came into your house. You did not give me any water for my feet, but she wet my feet with her tears and wiped them with her hair. You did not give me a kiss, but this woman, from the time I entered, has not stopped kissing my feet. You did not put oil on my head, but she has poured perfume on my feet. Therefore, I tell you, her many sins have been forgiven—for she loved much. But he who has been forgiven little loves little." (Luke 7:40-47)

Jesus tells a parable to help Simon see that he needs forgiveness just as much as the woman does. Simon has thoughtlessly neglected to welcome a well-known rabbi with water, a kiss, and oil. To omit this courtesy was to imply that Jesus was beneath Simon. Simon's judging of Jesus had begun before Jesus stepped through the door.[2] His self-righteousness clouds his vision of Jesus, the woman, and himself. His pride is as ugly as prostitution.

After telling the parable, Jesus turns to look at the woman. While looking at her, he says to Simon, "*Do you see this woman?*" Jesus wants Simon to stop judging and start looking. Simon knows only her past, but Jesus sees her present. Simon sees a category, but Jesus sees a changed person. Simon has a rigid view of people, one that places people in a category and keeps them there—blind men don't see and sinners don't repent.

Simon can't *see this woman* because he's filled with a sense of his own goodness. Strange as it seems, his good self-image prevents him from loving. His shock over this woman stems from the belief that (1) he would never do anything as bad as what she has done, and therefore (2) he is better than her, so (3) he doesn't

LOVE WALKED AMONG US

need anything Jesus might have to offer. Jesus' blunt parable and rebuke are directed at Simon's holier-than-thou attitude. ✳

When we are self-righteous, rigidity such as Simon's not only protects us, it also keeps our world from getting murky. When everything is clearly defined and everyone put in their place, with us as the righteous, we can relax. Sinners remind Pharisees that they are okay.

In rebuking Simon, Jesus empowers the woman. He defends her and honors her publicly. His praise of her becomes even more significant when we realize that he is honoring what first-century culture despised (women in general, prostitutes in particular) and he is despising what they honored (religious leaders). One rabbi was noted for his holiness because he threw stones at women who came near him in public!

Counter Cultural

By aligning himself with this woman, Jesus opened himself up to Simon's disdain. Jesus let her sins go, but in the process took on the stigma of her reputation. He paid a price to forgive her.

> *Then Jesus said to her, "Your sins are forgiven."*
> *The other guests began to say among themselves, "Who is this who even forgives sins?"*
> *Jesus said to the woman, "Your faith has saved you; go in peace." (Luke 7:48-50)*

Jesus completes her "healing" by forgiving her sins. When you've done something wrong, you want to be released from it. A conversation with the person you hurt helps, but sometimes that isn't possible. Jesus' forgiveness releases her.

Simon was crippled because he didn't see his proud heart, and thus his need for forgiveness. The woman, having seen the crippling effect of her sin and her need for forgiveness, simply needs to be welcomed. With her sins forgiven, her past forgotten, her dignity restored, she can *go in peace.* Just as the resurrection of the

53

dead son restored the widow to community, Jesus welcomes the woman into a new kind of community, one based on forgiveness.

Simon's guests are shocked. You might forgive someone who has hurt you, but you don't go around forgiving the sins of strangers. On another occasion when Jesus forgave a man's sins, the crowd responded, *"Why does this fellow talk like that? He's blaspheming! Who can forgive sins but God alone?"* (Mark 2:7). Jesus' extension of forgiveness, which they recognize as a claim to divinity, offends the guests. They are wondering, "Who does Jesus think he is? How can he forgive this woman?" Their reaction makes sense. If Sue hurts Joe, Joe might say to Sue, "I forgive you." But how can a stranger say to Sue, "I forgive you for what you did to Joe"? It's nonsense. But if all sin is ultimately against God, then Jesus' statement makes perfect sense—if he is God.

Jesus' compassion didn't lead him to whitewash the woman's sin. He took it seriously. With no hint of self-righteousness, Jesus brings a message of mercy to the woman and a message of rebuke for Simon. Usually we think of compassionate people as nice—they make good nurses, but they make lousy bill collectors. Yet Jesus is both compassionate and honest, with both Simon and the woman.

WE'RE ALL A MESS

In this next parable Jesus takes dead aim at self-righteousness:

> To some who were confident of their own righteousness and looked down on everybody else, Jesus told this parable: "Two men went up to the temple to pray, one a Pharisee and the other a tax collector. The Pharisee stood up and prayed about himself: 'God, I thank you that I am not like all other men—robbers, evildoers, adulterers—or even like this tax collector. I fast twice a week and give a tenth of all I get.'
>
> "But the tax collector stood at a distance. He would not even

look up to heaven, but beat his breast and said, 'God have mercy on me, a sinner.'

"I tell you that this man, rather than the other, went home justified before God. For everyone who exalts himself will be humbled, and he who humbles himself will be exalted." (Luke 18:9-14)

is this you?

This parable would have shocked Jesus' listeners. The Pharisee is truly a good guy—he recycles his trash, pays his bills, mows his lawn, gives money to charities, coaches baseball, doesn't beat his wife, and doesn't chase other women. He is John Q. Citizen at his very best.

On the other hand, the tax collector has sold out to the Roman government for money. He is the developer who puts in strip malls while ignoring the environment, the logger who clear-cuts virgin timber without reseeding, the stockbroker who advises you to sell just to make a commission. He doesn't so much disobey the law as use the law to line his own pockets. Every society has "tax collectors," and every society hates them.

But Jesus likes this tax collector better than the Pharisee because the tax collector sees what he really is—a mess—while the Pharisee denies his true heart. The point of the parable is clear: No one really has it all together. Everyone's life is a bit of a mess. All of us need help.

The Pharisee's arrogance overpowers his ability to see himself clearly. He just doesn't get it. But like the woman at Simon's house, the tax collector knows his life isn't working; he knows that his life has been centered on himself, playing God, running roughshod over people. He knows it and hates it, so he turns to outside help. He doesn't need just an assist from God; he needs a complete overhaul, so he cries out, *"God have mercy on me, a sinner."* He has come to the earth-shattering conclusion that he, not his circumstances, caused the mess in his life. Even his body language reflects his heart—he stands at a distance, not even looking up, beating his breast. He can't do life on his own anymore. Jesus finds this man's honesty more attractive than the proud accomplishments of the Pharisee.

Admitting Your Messiness

It is a huge relief to admit that you are a mess: that you turn inward and instinctively take care of your needs first. Try this little test by filling in the blanks of the Pharisee's prayer. It's a simple way to get in touch with your inner Pharisee.

> "God, I thank you that I am not like _____ (a group of people that drives you crazy) or even like _____ (one particular person who drives you crazy). I _____ (something good you do that those other people don't do)."

Knowing you are a mess means you can stop pretending you have it all together. Jesus says to people, "Relax—you're much worse than you think!"[3] It is a little scary to move in this direction because you lose control of your image—of how others see you. But did you ever control it anyway?

Jesus doesn't want his listeners to stay a mess; he wants them, like the tax collector, to turn to God and say, *"God have mercy on me, a sinner."* Getting in touch with your inner tax collector makes room for God's energy in your life. Jesus concludes the parable saying: *"I tell you that this man, rather than the other, went home justified before God."* The first step toward God is realizing you are on the wrong path going the wrong way. It's actually quite freeing if you think about it. With your mask off you can get real and relax.

When we realize that we don't have it all together, we can care for people because we no longer feel morally superior to them. Consequently, we are quicker to help than to give advice, quicker to listen than to lecture. Observing the tenderness that poured out of the woman, Jesus told Simon, *"she loved much."* But he also observed the coldness of Simon: *"He who has been forgiven little loves little."*

According to Jesus, we all need forgiveness. Knowing we are inadequate before God and other people leads to compassion, but thinking we are good before God and others makes us self-centered and difficult to live with. The better we think we are, the less we can love. The more we see our need, the more we'll turn for help . . . and the more we'll help others because we are able to see their need.

tough chapter!

CHAPTER FIVE

"THIS IS WHAT YOU SHOULD DO"

LEGALISM BLOCKS COMPASSION

I N PENNSYLVANIA WE STILL HAVE "BLUE laws" on the books that say you can't purchase a flashlight on Sunday if you are going to use it for fishing, but you can buy a flashlight if you use it to look at a sore throat. My family had a similar rule when I was growing up. I could read only religious books on Sundays. Sundays were a day of rest when you only thought about God.

Legalism takes a good rule—such as "rest one day a week"—and creates a rigid system that forgets about people. Just as judging and self-righteousness block compassion, so can legalism. Legalism reinforces self-righteousness because it communicates to you the good news of your own goodness. It systematizes judging, eliminating gray areas so we don't have to think about love.

How Legalism Works

We get a window into how legalism works by watching Jesus at the home of another Pharisee:

When Jesus had finished speaking, a Pharisee invited him to eat with him; so he went in and reclined at the table. But the Pharisee, noticing that Jesus did not first wash before the meal, was surprised.

Then the Lord [Jesus] said to him, "Now then, you Pharisees clean the outside of the cup and dish, but inside you are full of greed and wickedness. You foolish people! Did not the one who made the outside make the inside also? But give what is inside the dish to the poor, and everything will be clean for you.

"Woe to you Pharisees, because you give God a tenth of your mint, rue, and all other kinds of garden herbs, but you neglect justice and the love of God. You should have practiced the latter without leaving the former undone.

"Woe to you Pharisees, because you love the most important seats in the synagogues and the greetings in the marketplaces."
(*Luke 11:37-43*)

All the Pharisee wanted Jesus to do was wash his hands before he ate. Why is Jesus so upset? Jesus is reacting to a legalist ritual that permeated Jewish culture, and in turn, blocked love. Every time they washed their hands the Pharisees heard the good news: "I'm better than people who don't wash."

Jesus lambastes the Pharisees for appearing to be one way, but being another. They would scrupulously *give God a tenth of their mint, rue, and all the other garden herbs,* but then neglect the poor. They would appear one way in public and another in private because they were only concerned about how they looked in front of their group. Jesus tells them, *"You love the most important seats."* On another occasion he described the Pharisees: *"Everything they do is done for men to see"* (*Matthew 23:5*). Legalists want people to look at them, while those who love look at others.

Because the legalist derives his worth as a person from other people's opinions, legalism functions like a false god, giving organization and identity to a person's life. The ancient Near East was

LOVE WALKED AMONG US

a shame-honor culture that constantly measured people by their conformity to the social rules of their particular group—Roman, Greek, or Jewish. Knowing the rules, the codes of the culture, makes us acceptable. That's why the Pharisees clung so tenaciously to their rules, their codes of culture. Our culture clings to rules in the same way: Women must have a fulfilling career while they raise perfect children and look awesome. Men have to do all that and be sensitive and charming as well. Our legalism leaves us exhausted as a culture.

Jesus goes to the heart of the problem when he says, *"You Pharisees clean the outside of the cup and dish, but inside you are full of greed and wickedness."* He's referring to the Pharisees' practice of only using cups and dishes that were ritually clean. He uses this ritual as a metaphor for what is wrong with legalism: What good does it do to clean the outside of the cup if the inside is filthy? A focus on outer goodness masks inner badness—people's hearts are bad, not just their actions.

Legalism doesn't produce love because it doesn't deal with bad motivations. It assumes that the inside of the cup is basically good, and if people would just "do" the right thing, then everything will be okay. Rules, by themselves, can provide great comfort because it appears that we can attain them by ourselves. But for Jesus, that's the problem—"ourselves." Unless you deal with "self"—with human ego—focusing on rules is like rearranging the deck chairs on the Titanic while it is sinking. **pointless!**

The Real Problem

After criticizing the Pharisees for their legalistic eating rituals, Jesus explains more fully why legalism doesn't work—there is an evil bent in us:

"Listen to me, everyone, and understand this. Nothing outside a man can make him 'unclean' by going into him. Rather, it is what comes out of a man that makes him 'unclean'. . . . For from within, out of men's hearts, come evil thoughts, sexual immorality, theft, murder, adultery, greed, malice, deceit, lewdness, envy, slander, arrogance and folly. All these evils come from inside and make a man 'unclean.'" (Mark 7:14-15,21-23)

To test the accuracy of Jesus' assessment, take a notepad to work or family gathering and jot down your thoughts—good and bad—about others. Every criticism, every fear, every compassion, every jealousy. Be honest about what you are really thinking. Then shred it!

Jesus believed that the world is beautiful, but broken. People were created to live a life of love, but became broken. We are like an exquisite Japanese vase shattered on the ground—you can still see the beauty in the individual shards, but everywhere you look, it's broken. It's true. Everywhere, we see beauty and brokenness, love and hate, giving and greed. Everything cries out for something better.

If evil is an intrusion, then it is potentially fixable. There is room for hope. But if what is wrong with our world is "natural," then we're in trouble—we're like an old Dodge I had that was constantly stalling in the middle of intersections. If something is intrinsically wrong with us—if we're lemons like my old Dodge—then we need to be junked. That was Freud's view: "I have found little that is 'good' about human beings on the whole. In my experience most of them are trash."[1] Freud held out little hope for humankind. But Jesus came proclaiming good news: God was going to destroy evil through him.

Jesus told the bad news so that people could hear the good. For instance, when the tax collector (in the parable about the Tax Collector and the Pharisee) saw the bad news about himself, he was able to stop pretending, and so God forgave him. But the Pharisee, fooled by legalism about his own goodness, didn't think

LOVE WALKED AMONG US

he needed forgiveness, and so he didn't receive it. <u>Our helplessness is the door to the knowledge of God.</u> Without changing the heart, obsessing over rules is like spray-painting garbage.

Day-to-Day Legalism

We can see the subtlety of legalism in this story of Mary and Martha, good friends of Jesus:

> *As Jesus and his disciples were on their way, he came to a village where a woman named Martha opened her home to him. She had a sister called Mary, who sat at the Lord's feet listening to what he said. But Martha was distracted by all the preparations that had to be made. She came to him and asked, "Lord, don't you care that my sister has left me to do the work by myself? Tell her to help me!"*
>
> *"Martha, Martha," the Lord answered, "you are worried and upset about many things, but only one thing is needed. Mary has chosen what is better, and it will not be taken away from her."*
> *(Luke 10:38-42)*

Task-oriented Martha focuses on work. It's likely that she is the eldest child, since she invites Jesus to dinner and it's her home. She also has a typical first child's personality: competent, take-charge, and responsible. Martha's rule is simple: You honor an esteemed guest by <u>preparing a meal.</u>

Her sister Mary is <u>people-oriented.</u> She wants to hear what Jesus is talking about. Not only has Mary left Martha with all the work, but she's just sitting there, doing nothing, <u>enjoying the conversation.</u> — relax *"Sitting at the feet"* is also the Hebrew expression for a rabbi's disciple (a position reserved exclusively for men. Rabbis thought it was a sin to teach a woman.)[2]

In Martha's eyes Mary should not be acting like a disciple—she should be helping in the kitchen, not out with the men. As the

63

steam builds, Martha begins to see that Jesus, Mr. Know-It-All-Rabbi, is the real problem. How could he let Mary get away with this? Doesn't he know this is the first century? Has he forgotten all the rules?

Like all of Jesus' close friends Martha has a blunt, forthright honesty. She doesn't keep her thoughts to herself the way Simon did, nor does she care what Jesus thinks about her as she reproves him for a lack of compassion: *"Don't you care. . . ?"*

A good principle dominates Martha's mind: "sharing." We should help one another. But legalism takes bits and pieces of good things and uses them as weapons. Martha sees only the principle, not the person. She doesn't act confused—she is quite confident—but her self-righteousness has confused her. Simon only saw the woman's adulterous past; Martha only sees her pile of dishes. Clinging to a good rule blinds her to Mary and to Jesus, and makes Martha abrasive. Legalism flows from and feeds self-righteousness. It doesn't "look" because it has figured everything out ahead of time.

Just as he protected the adulterous woman and the blind man, Jesus defends Mary by gently, but bluntly, exposing Martha's restlessness. In the midst of all her to-do lists, her hustle and bustle, Martha has lost a quiet center. Jesus gently suggests that *one thing is needed*—sitting at his feet. There, at his feet, she can find inner rest.

Legalism Hides Selfishness

We meet Mary again six days before Jesus' death. Mary, Martha, and their brother, Lazarus, invite Jesus over to dinner.

> *Six days before the Passover, Jesus arrived at Bethany, where Lazarus lived, whom Jesus had raised from the dead. Here a dinner was given in Jesus' honor. Martha served, while Lazarus was among those reclining at the table with him. Then Mary took about a pint of pure nard, an expensive perfume; she poured it on Jesus' feet*

LOVE WALKED AMONG US

and wiped his feet with her hair. And the house was filled with the fragrance of the perfume.

But one of his disciples, Judas Iscariot, who was later to betray him, objected, "Why wasn't this perfume sold and the money given to the poor? It was worth a year's wages." He did not say this because he cared about the poor but because he was a thief; as keeper of the money bag, he used to help himself to what was put into it.

"Leave her alone," Jesus replied. "It was intended that she should save this perfume for the day of my burial. You will always have the poor among you, but you will not always have me."
(John 12:1-8)

The perfume is almost certainly her dowry. If so, she is giving up marriage and children for these few moments of lavishing her love on Jesus. The cost of her gift suggests the extent of her love. Each time we meet Mary in the Gospels, she is at Jesus' feet, either listening, weeping, or worshiping. Martha hasn't missed a beat— she is still serving. Judas has taken over her old role of grumbling.

Judas hides behind a good principle: "give to the poor." A denarius is a day's wage for a working person, so Mary has just dumped about $25,000 down the drain—all over Jesus. Judas' legalism tells him that he is a good person, hiding his greed and hatred even from himself. It sounds altruistic and spiritual to advocate giving money to the poor, but Judas had been embezzling the money he was supposedly keeping safe.

True to form, Jesus defends Mary's passionate outpouring of love against Judas' oppressive, legalistic hypocrisy. He protects Mary by rebuking Judas, thus honoring her in the same way he honored the "sinful" woman in Simon's house.

Who Will Pay for the Video?

We can easily spot Judas and Martha's legalism, but identifying our own is not so simple. I know.

Jill manages our money, but I had saved a little on the side for going out to lunch. I was getting tired of peanut butter and jelly sandwiches. (I hadn't recovered from the time when Jill, in a fit of managerial madness, had made and frozen thirty peanut butter and jelly sandwiches at the beginning of the week to simplify lunch preparation for the rest of the week!)

It was Saturday evening so Jill and I rented a movie. No big deal. We had been tight financially, so when the time came to take the movie back, she wanted me to pay for it out of my nest egg and not the family budget. I thought she was being greedy, and we argued about who would pay for the three-dollar rental.

As I thought about our little spat, I realized that my good rule (you shouldn't be greedy) combined with my sense of being right, led me to quarrel over three dollars. For starters I had forgotten that I had agreed to pay for the movie. But regardless, my legalism—as all legalism does—communicated to Jill that she had less value than the price of a video rental.

I have a tough time seeing my own legalism because my rules seem so good and so true—I didn't have a lot of money in my stash, and it is good to share. But good and true things blind the legalist. Like Judas my appeal to sharing hid my own greed and was an attempt to transfer guilt in the name of virtue.

The Peculiar Blindness of the Legalist

Did you notice that in each of these accounts the accusing person had the same problem he or she is judging in the other person? The self-righteous legalist gets irritated at others but is guilty of the same faults.

Martha accuses Jesus of not caring, but Martha hasn't cared

for Jesus or for her sister. She can't enjoy the fact that her work frees up Mary to learn from Jesus. Instead of quietly asking for help, she judges Jesus for the very thing she is doing. Simon judges Jesus for being insensitive and blind when he is the one who is thoughtless and can't see. And like Martha, I saw myself as the victim: "Jill manages our money, and I only have this little bit." But the very thing I accused Jill of (being tight-fisted) was motivating me. We are remarkably perceptive of others' shortcomings and sins, but curiously blind to our own. We see others' problems and rigidity, but not our own. Jesus said, "All these evils come from inside" (Mark 7:23). Consequently, we don't like others looking at us, for fear that they'll discover what's inside.

Jean-Paul Sartre, the French philosopher, said that one of the most unnerving things that can happen to you is to be looking through a peephole at someone, only to realize the other person is looking at you.[3]

Jesus sees right through people. This has been true for many who have studied him. It's both wonderful and scary at the same time. Scary because we don't particularly like someone else looking through our peephole at us; yet wonderful because there is something magnetic about truth. Did you ever wonder why in horror movies the person opens the door to find out what the noise is? We're all thinking, "Don't open the door. There is something awful on the other side." But truth draws like a magnet—especially when the truth-teller is Jesus.

On Jesus' last trip to Jerusalem, Mark observes this same reaction to Jesus, a reaction of fear and wonder: *They were on their way up to Jerusalem, with Jesus leading the way, and the disciples were astonished, while those who followed were afraid* (Mark 10:32).

I wonder if that is what it feels like to be around a king— a real king with old-fashioned chop-off-their-heads kind of authority. Except this king is really gentle: so though you'd still be a little nervous around him, you'd feel very safe with him too. He is good. Not tame. Not predictable. Not controllable. But good.

CHAPTER SIX

THE GOLDEN RULE

INCARNATION LEADS TO COMPASSION

I ENJOY BEING CHEAP. I USED TO THINK I WAS just frugal, but now I frankly admit it is not a virtue. I like to find the exact change so I don't have to break a five-dollar bill. An inner contentment comes over me when I get a free movie at Blockbuster with a coupon. The amount of money is not crucial—it just feels good to save. I am the same with efficiency. I love it. I've caught myself spending ten minutes figuring out how to do something more efficiently when the task only takes five minutes. I tell you all this to help you understand what I am going to tell you next.

I went to my daughter Ashley's game to watch her play. She had played very hard, working up a tremendous thirst. As she came off the field, I told her what a great job she had done. She said, "I am so thirsty, Dad, could you get me a soda?" My initial reaction was to give her some of the ice water that was reserved for players. It was cheap and efficient.

But then I put myself in Ashley's shoes: "She's tired. She's played a hard game, and she wants a soda, not a glass of water. I can do that. I have money in my pocket. I could spend that money." I even stuck a hand in my pocket and felt my change. "I could walk over to the soda machine several hundred yards away in the school building and get a soda for Ashley. Paul, this won't kill you." This is truly what went through my mind. I went to the soda machine with a little kick in my step, partly because I envisioned how Ashley's face would brighten when I handed her the soda.

Because I'm not naturally compassionate, I had to stop and "think Ashley." It only took a couple of seconds, but at each step I encountered little beliefs (frugality, efficiency) that can block compassion. To move inside Ashley's world I had to leave my own behind.

If I hadn't been studying Jesus and how he loved people, it would never have occurred to me to do this. But I had noticed how Jesus thought as he loved people. Let me show you what I mean.

> *During those days another large crowd gathered. Since they had noth-*
> *ing to eat, Jesus called his disciples to him and said, "I have compassion*
> *for these people; they have already been with me three days and have*
> *nothing to eat. If I send them home hungry, they will collapse on the*
> *way, because some of them have come a long distance." (Mark 8:1-3)*

Jesus makes three observations—*they have been with me three days, have nothing to eat,* and *have come a long distance*—and concludes *if I send them home hungry, they will collapse.* Why even mention these observations? I think it's because nothing is obvious if it's not happening to you. With these words, Jesus shows us that love takes work: he has to slow down, put himself in the crowd's shoes, and think about their needs. Love requires that we forget our own needs in order to think about someone else.

This is "incarnation"—it comes from the Latin "in carnes" and means, literally, "in the flesh." Jesus "incarnates" with the crowd— he walks in their shoes—by thinking about their situation. Then he feeds them by miraculously multiplying a few loaves and fish.

Another time, instead of looking at a crowd's physical needs, Jesus "incarnates" by looking at their emotional state: *"When he saw the crowds, he had compassion on them, because they were harassed and helpless, like sheep without a shepherd"* (Matthew 9:36).

Sheep are a complete mess without a shepherd. They get lost or they might overeat. If they turn the wrong way when they are lying down, they will end up "cast" on their backs, unable to right themselves. You hear about wild dogs, wild cats, or wild goats, but you never hear about "wild sheep" — they need constant care. Jesus wasn't fooled by appearances because he walked in the crowd's shoes. Because of this he could see their confusion, loneliness, and helplessness. Incarnation leads to compassion.

How Do We Incarnate?

How do you get "inside of someone"? The Golden Rule, Jesus' famous summary of love, gives us a hint: *"Do to others as you would have them do to you"* (Luke 6:31). First ask yourself, "What would I like someone to do for me in that situation?" Then go and do that for the person. Think, then do. Using our natural tendency toward self-preoccupation, Jesus gently turns self-awareness on its head. The Golden Rule is a simple prescription for "unselfing." When Jesus saw the large crowd he stopped, thought about their needs, and then acted.

Our son John was having a hard time. He was disorganized, mouthy, and miserable—in other words, a typical thirteen-year-old. Jill and I tried every imaginable form of restriction or encouragement, but nothing seemed to be working. We were becoming more concerned.

Then, instead of looking at him from a parent's perspective, I thought about what his life was like. He was an above average student with below average grades. He didn't like traditional sports, which meant he wasn't part of the in-group of guys. When he woke up in the morning, he didn't have much to feel good about or to

71

look forward to. When things got hard he couldn't say, "At least I am good at _____."

I realized that John needed a little kick in his step—something that would allow him to hold his head high. I chewed on this for about a week. I thought about his strengths. He's quick and strong, and I thought he might enjoy wrestling; so I asked him if he'd enjoy wrestling. He was interested so I asked the athletic director if the school might be interested in starting a team. He said yes, so we scrounged together some mats and money for a coach.

But then we couldn't find a coach—so good old Dad volunteered. Since I knew nothing about wrestling, I went to the library and pored over wrestling books. Fortunately, at the last minute, we found a real coach. John went on to get MVP twice and to become team captain. By his sophomore year, he could pin me in about ten seconds. His junior year I just stayed away from him whenever he looked menacing.

Love is more than listening or being kind. It needs to be thoughtful. It needs to be shaped by the person's need. John's varsity wrestling jacket did more for him than a thousand "I love yous" or hours of sympathetic listening ever would have. And so did my support. John will forever remember me sitting on the living room floor with a book in one hand, trying to figure out wrestling moves.

DIFFERENT PEOPLE, DIFFERENT RESPONSES

Jesus shapes his love to the person. When Martha and Mary are grieving over the death of their brother Lazarus, both sisters tell Jesus, *"If you had been here, my brother would not have died"* (John 11:21,32). With Martha, Jesus discusses the possibility of the resurrection. But with Mary, he looks at her and weeps.

Why, in identical situations, is Jesus different?

Because they are different people. Martha is more aggressive and task-oriented; Mary is more trusting and people-oriented.

LOVE WALKED AMONG US

With Martha Jesus responds by talking with her about hope and trust, but he joins Mary in sorrow and then acts to raise her brother. Two different people, two different responses.

Jesus doesn't blindly follow some "rule" that prescribes how we should relate to people who are in pain. His love is not a system of do's and don'ts that tries to shape people. Each person is different; consequently Jesus shapes his response to what the person is like.

Lynette, a friend of mine, went to visit her father who was dying of cancer. She was dreading the visit because he was an old-fashioned male chauvinist. When she arrived, he was upset with their bridge-playing friends. He told her that they had all agreed to each contribute $10 a week toward a trip they were planning to take. He didn't think he would join them because of the advanced state of his cancer, and he felt he was wasting his money on his friends. Lynette's first thought was to tell him, "What are you going to do, take the money with you when you die? You are so selfish." She wanted to tell him to stop being greedy — in other words, to give him a good rule to straighten him out.

But instead, she phoned his friends and explained her father's concern. They were understanding and agreed that he shouldn't contribute to the common pot. Instead of trying to solve her Dad's problems with a quick dose of truth, Lynette got her hands dirty, took some time, and helped in the specifics.

Some people might think she should stand up to her father and stop enabling him. Others may think that Lynette is not being honest by not dealing with her father's selfishness. But Lynette's love for her father was shaped by his need. She didn't "lose her personality" by entering into her dad's world. She felt his fear and sensed his desire for his friends to acknowledge that he was not going to be around much longer. Her practical love for her dad wasn't dishonest.

Love adjusts to different people without losing your own identity. That is what incarnation is all about.

Top-Down Versus Bottom-Up

We see the same pattern in Jesus' encounter with a blind man sitting by the gates of Jericho.

> *When he heard that it was Jesus of Nazareth, he began to shout, "Jesus, Son of David, have mercy on me!" Many rebuked him and told him to be quiet, but he shouted all the more, "Son of David, have mercy on me!"*
>
> *Jesus stopped and said, "Call him."*
>
> *So they called to the blind man, "Cheer up! On your feet! He's calling you." Throwing his cloak aside, he jumped to his feet and came to Jesus.*
>
> *"What do you want me to do for you?" Jesus asked him.*
>
> *The blind man said, "Rabbi, I want to see."*
>
> *"Go," said Jesus, "your faith has healed you." Immediately he received his sight and followed Jesus along the road.*
> (Mark 10:47-52)

The blind man had heard about Jesus' healing power. He'd also heard that Jesus is a descendant of the ancient Israelite king, David. He is the promised one, a king with power to change things. But Jesus doesn't act like a powerful person. Instead, he takes the time to ask the blind man what he wants. Shouldn't this be obvious? Why not just heal the man and get on to the next beggar? But for a brief moment Jesus goes inside the blind man's skin. Asking questions slows us down and puts us in other people's worlds, hearing their words, their expressions, and their desires. We become the learner rather than the expert.

Jesus' question, *"What do you want me to do for you?"* is not as obvious as we might think. Once Jesus asked a crippled man, *"Do you want to get well?"* (John 5:6), and the man answered with a long whine. Evidently his illness gave him an identity that he cherished more than healing. Sometimes our problems do that for us.

We patronize people when we assume that we know how they want to be helped. If we don't ask, we may heal the blind man, but he might not feel loved, only fixed. This is "top-down" love. Though we may sincerely want to help, we are trying to do so from a superior position, with little risk to ourselves. Instead of considering how we can love people with their weaknesses, we consider how they should be different—often we think they should be like us.

Top-down love decides how and when to love. But when our love is bottom-up, we lose control of how to love. Others decide for us. Bottom-up love is the best kind of love because no one can help me think about your world better than you can.

A word of caution: Don't be legalistic about asking questions. Jesus didn't always ask people if they wanted to be healed. At times he even tested people, making it difficult for them to get to him. Jesus' life doesn't give us a "love formula." Religion and pop psychology often reduce love to specific behaviors (for example, "always ask questions"), thus simplifying love so we don't have to work at it. We like clarity. "Just tell me what to do." But Jesus deals with people as they are.

WHO WILL MAKE THE FIRST MOVE?

What if everyone did this? What if everywhere you went, people would be concerned about you, thinking about you. It sounds good, until we think about who will make the first move. If we follow the Golden Rule, there is no guarantee that we will be treated the same in return. No one knows this better than Jesus. As he was dying on the cross, *the chief priests and the teachers of the law mocked him among themselves. "He saved others," they said, "but he can't save himself!"* (Mark 15:31).

Not only did Jesus incarnate in many small instances, but his whole life was an incarnation. Calling Jesus *the Word*, John puts it this way in his gospel: *In the beginning was the Word, and the Word was with God, and the Word was God. . . . The Word became flesh and made his dwelling among us* (John 1:1,14). John came to the startling conclusion that Jesus was God in the flesh. If so, God didn't just *think* about putting on our shoes—he wore them by becoming a person.

The question, "Who will make the first move?" is answered. God did.

PART 2
LOVE SPEAKS THE TRUTH

CHAPTER SEVEN

A TIME TO SPEAK UP

BALANCING COMPASSION
WITH HONESTY

ESUS SHOCKED ME WHEN I READ THE GOSPELS. I FOUND his honesty and forthrightness to be relentless, almost rude. How could someone who was so compassionate treat people this way?

Think back, for example, to how he treated Simon. Yes, Simon insulted him—he doesn't greet Jesus with a kiss, wash his feet, or pour oil on his head—but most people would have more problems with the woman's public display of affection. But Jesus tells Simon that this marriage-wrecker is doing a better job of loving than he is . . . and he does it in front of the man's guests!

People just don't do that kind of thing when they are someone's guests—in any culture, in any period of history. Rather than address a public insult directly, we usually complain to our friends about it. But Jesus doesn't gossip. He speaks directly to his host in front of everyone, as if he doesn't care what Simon thinks of him.

If we'd been in Jesus' shoes, we might have worried that people would get the wrong idea about our relationship with the woman. Or about what she might think. After all, overly emotional people don't have the normal social barriers the rest of us have. Maybe she'll be like a leech, sucking up all our energy. If we open the door a crack, she'll stick her whole foot through. Others might reject us if we take her side.

Not Jesus. He's committed to truth at all costs. It was wrong for Simon to judge the woman. It was wrong for Simon to judge Jesus. And it was wrong for Simon to greet Jesus the way he did. Yet Simon's immoral behavior is being masqueraded as goodness, and Jesus wants no part of the charade. To remain silent would be the same as endorsing his behavior.

IMPORTANCE OF TRUTH IN RELATIONSHIPS

Jesus knows we need to be both compassionate and honest in our relationships. He told his followers to have an honesty that moves toward people. *"If your brother sins against you, go and show him his fault, just between the two of you"* (Matthew 18:15). Without that honesty, our relationships get weird.

Here are two everyday examples that capture how important truth is in a relationship.

Allison had left some dishes in the sink. Her husband criticized her cleaning, saying, "Why the ___ is this in the sink?" Crushed and wounded, Allison shut down for several days. This wasn't the first time he'd sworn at her, and she told me that she was thinking of leaving him. I urged her to tell him honestly how she felt when he spoke to her that way. Reluctantly, she braved his anger and told him what he had done and why it was wrong. Surprised that his words bothered her, he said, "That's how I treat everyone." But he heard her, and began to consciously work on his harshness.

Alan's wife had not gone to the dentist during their entire marriage. Occasionally he would express his desire that she go. She finally did, and, as expected, needed major dental work, including several extractions. Afterward, she accused Alan of keeping her from going. A friend told Alan, "You've got to tell her what she has done by blaming you for her refusal to go the dentist. It's just not right. She may not like it, but she needs your honesty, regardless of how she receives it." He hesitated, not wanting to hurt her. But if we abandon truth telling, we allow people to hurt themselves or others with their own willfulness. Each of us can easily slip into an isolated, self-righteous life unless we're confronted with truth.

JESUS' COMMITMENT TO TRUTH

Not only is he committed to truth, Jesus fearlessly risks his reputation for truth. His boldness and commitment to justice both have a stark, uncompromising quality that leaves people uncomfortable. Watch how this unfolds when Jesus visits the home of a prominent Pharisee after a Sabbath synagogue service:

> When he noticed how the guests picked the places of honor at the table, he told them this parable: "When someone invites you to a wedding feast, do not take the place of honor, for a person more distinguished than you may have been invited. If so, the host who invited both of you will come and say to you, 'Give this man your seat.' Then, humiliated, you will have to take the least important place. But when you are invited, take the lowest place, so that when your host comes, he will say to you, 'Friend, move up to a better place.' Then you will be honored in the presence of all your fellow guests. For everyone who exalts himself will be humbled, and he who humbles himself will be exalted." (Luke 14:7-11)

Every culture ranks people, and here Jesus again upsets the cultural norm. When guests in someone's home, we might notice something that isn't quite right, but usually we mention it quietly to our spouse or friends on the way home. But Jesus tells everyone present that in taking the seats of honor, they have displayed arrogance and pride.

If I had a good seat at that banquet, I'd be pleased with myself. If I had a bad seat, I would notice the pride in those who got the good seats. But Jesus, who is likely the guest of honor at this banquet, is not concerned about being prominent, nor is he intimidated by those who are. Instead of hiding behind his prominence, he risks his reputation to teach the guests about love. He uses a superior position to teach them not to seek for position. Jesus always uses his power to help people.

But Jesus isn't finished. He tells the host that he has invited all the wrong people.

> *Then Jesus said to his host, "When you give a luncheon or a dinner, do not invite your friends, your brothers or relatives, or your rich neighbors; if you do, they may invite you back and so you will be repaid. But when you give a banquet, invite the poor, the crippled, the lame, the blind, and you will be blessed. Although they cannot repay you, you will be repaid at the resurrection of the righteous."* (Luke 14:12-14)

Jesus' honesty cuts right to the quick. His comments affirm these two standards of morality:

1. Don't be motivated by pride or power. If you are, one day you will be brought low.
2. Don't think you are loving just because you are kind to people—it might be a secret way of getting something for yourself. The real test of kindness is if you give to people who can't repay you in any way—even by telling others about how good you are.

LOVE WALKED AMONG US

Jesus is saying that when we seek out the least enjoyable person at the office party, the person who has so little to give, God notices. God will repay us *at the resurrection of the righteous* for showing kindness to outcasts. In other words, the universe is connected in ways that we can't see. The hidden behavior of love—and genuine love is usually hidden—is ultimately recognized by God. Love counts to God.

When Jesus was just eight days old, Mary and Joseph presented him at the temple in Jerusalem as prescribed by the Torah, the Jewish book of the law. An old man, Simeon, met them, took the infant Jesus in his arms, and said that through this little boy, ". . . *the thoughts of many hearts will be revealed" (Luke 2:35)*. Two thousand years later, Jesus' words still reveal our thoughts.

FREEDOM FROM OPINIONS

Jesus has a strong commitment to what is right and the courage to express it. Like the ancient Hebrew prophets, he is utterly fearless. Others don't control his behavior. He calls power-hungry Herod, the ruler of Galilee, a *"fox."* He calls the hypocritical Pharisees *"whitewashed graves"* and a *"brood of snakes" (Luke 13:32; Matthew 23:27,33)*.

The Pharisees actually praise Jesus for not being swayed by people's opinions. It's the only compliment they ever give him.

> *Then the Pharisees went out and laid plans to trap him in his words. They sent their disciples to him. . . . "Teacher," they said, "we know you are a man of integrity and that you teach the way of God in accordance with the truth. You aren't swayed by men, because you pay no attention to who they are. Tell us then, what is your opinion? Is it right to pay taxes to Caesar or not?"*
>
> *But Jesus, knowing their evil intent said, "You hypocrites, why are you trying to trap me? Show me the coin used for paying the tax." They brought him a denarius, and he asked them, "Whose*

portrait is this? And whose inscription?"

"Caesar's," they replied.

Then he said to them, "Give to Caesar what is Caesar's, and to God what is God's."

When they heard this, they were amazed. So they left him and went away. (Matthew 22:15-22)

Ironically, their praise for his honesty is dishonest. Knowing this, Jesus responds with brutal candor, exposing their motivation *(Why are you trying to trap me?)* and what their hearts are like *(hypocrites)*.

Jesus' soul is anchored in God; this frees him from other people's opinions. In another conversation with the Pharisees, he says, *"I do not accept praise from men, but I know you. I know that you do not have the love of God in your hearts. . . . How can you believe if you accept praise from one another, yet make no effort to obtain the praise that comes from the only God?" (John 5:41-42,44)*. Jesus' God-consciousness explains his extraordinary behavior. He knows God is watching, enjoying, and loving him. Because he has *the love of God in his heart,* he doesn't need other people to love him.

Picture what the world would be like if no one had hidden agendas—everything out on the table, no gossip or talking behind people's backs. Imagine how freeing it would be to live like Jesus, not ruled by people's opinions, to only be concerned about God's view of us, thus freeing us to care for others with honest words that lead either to rejection or genuine closeness.

Most of us don't live this way. We get consumed with how we come across to people. We hunger for their approval and become manipulative. This creates a false, but fleeting, sense of satisfaction. Or, we judge others, telling them that they need our approval. But Jesus describes a new way to care for people, one unconcerned with their opinion of us, one in which we have both compassion and candor, making our relationships real. Jesus said: *"He who speaks on his own does so to gain honor for himself, but he who works for the honor*

LOVE WALKED AMONG US

of the one who sent him is a man of truth; there is nothing false about him" (*John 7:18*).

THE DISCIPLES' HONESTY

Truthfulness characterized every relationship Jesus had. He enjoys honesty in others, even at his own expense. Watch how he interacts with Nathanael when they first meet:

> *The next day Jesus decided to leave for Galilee. Finding Philip, he said to him, "Follow me."*
>
> *Philip, like Andrew and Peter, was from the town of Bethsaida. Philip found Nathanael and told him, "We have found the one Moses wrote about in the Law, and about whom the prophets also wrote—Jesus of Nazareth, the son of Joseph."*
>
> *"Nazareth! Can anything good come from there?" Nathanael asked.*
>
> *"Come and see," said Philip.*
>
> *When Jesus saw Nathanael approaching, he said of him, "Here is a true Israelite, in whom there is nothing false."*
>
> *"How do you know me?" asked Nathanael.*
>
> *Jesus answered, "I saw you while you were still under the fig tree before Philip called you." (John 1:43-48)*

In one brief sentence Nathanael dismisses Jesus' mother, family, relatives, childhood friends, and everyone else from his hometown! But he's also forthright and honest, open to correction. Jesus not only ignores the dig, but he also commends Nathanael's bluntness, calling him *a true Israelite, in whom there is nothing false.* Jesus enjoys people who tell it like it is. Most of the disciples shared this quality.

Several weeks before Jesus' death, James and John, both in the inner circle, use their mom to make a power play:

A TIME TO SPEAK UP

Then the mother of Zebedee's sons came to Jesus with her sons and, kneeling down, asked a favor of him.

"What is it you want?" he asked.

She said, "Grant that one of these two sons of mine may sit at your right and the other at your left in your kingdom."

(Matthew 20:20-21)

Their bid for power is so blatant, it's charming—getting your mother to go to bat for you with the boss! Most adults would never do that sort of thing. Or would we? Perhaps we aren't so overt, but we might act out the same desires secretly, manipulating to get ahead. James and John's ambitions are out on the table for all to see. They have a childlike, straightforward honesty—they were real.

Taking Off the Mask (Becoming Real)

The word "hypocrite" is the Greek word for "actor." Jesus' home-town of Nazareth was three miles south of the city of Sepphoris, which was being built while Jesus was working as a carpenter or builder. He most likely worked there. Perhaps Jesus went to the Greek theater in Sepphoris and noticed the similarity between the "hypocrites" with their masks and the people around him. Jesus challenged those around him to stop performing—literally. He encouraged people to take off their masks.

A mask puts on a false face and conceals our true face, but those close to us can see the mask. I saw this one Monday night when Courtney was home from college for Ashley's birthday. I had moved an appointment later in the evening in order to take Courtney back to college—about forty-five minutes away. She and I agreed to leave by seven o'clock so I could get to my appointment in time.

After our little party I bathed and dressed Kimberly so she

was ready for bed. Emily, our sixth child, was whining. I felt like I had a flu bug coming on, and I was tired. Seven o'clock came and Courtney was still upstairs. I told her that I needed to go, explaining that I had already moved my appointment once. We finally left, and on the way out the door I turned to Jill and said, "Would you call my appointment to tell them I will be late?" It was just a simple request for Jill. But my appointment really didn't care if I was late, and by saying what I did in front of Courtney, I indirectly blamed her for causing me a problem. That was wrong. Not surprisingly, Courtney got irritated at me. I was manipulating her while appearing nice.

We show our hearts in how we act in life's private incidents, not the public ones. Jesus said, *"Whoever can be trusted with very little can also be trusted with much, and whoever is dishonest with very little will also be dishonest with much"* (Luke 16:10).

What was really going on inside me? On the outside I was tired and weary, and I had already changed my appointment once to help Courtney. But inside I was thinking about how good I was to help Courtney by taking her back to school, and that she owed me something for my kindness. My unspoken rule was: "You should be nice to me, because I am nice to you."

I was the Pharisee: criticizing Courtney for making me late, when I was only thinking about myself. I wasn't concerned about my appointment—only that my "on time" rule had been broken. Looking back, I should have just canceled my appointment. It wasn't that important. If it had been, I could have gone upstairs, seen Courtney reading to Emily, and told her about it. Then I could have quietly called the appointment to say I was going to be late. No manipulation needed.

THE GIFT OF HONESTY

Our culture would like to have a formless compassion without rules. But even that is a rule. We simply can't escape rules. The Golden Rule is, after all, a rule. Earlier, we saw Jesus react to people who misuse rules; now we see him react to people who neglect rules.

We instinctively know that Jesus is right about hypocrisy. It's just plain wrong to wear a mask—to pretend you care for women's rights but belittle your wife, to pretend you care for the environment but throw trash out the car window.

If only car wrecks and cancer plagued this world, compassion would be all we need. We would not need to be truth-tellers. But our world also has abusive husbands and mean wives; it has thieves and liars, murderers and adulterers. We are broken, both physically and morally.

Jesus shows us that without truth, our relationships lack definition and meaning. If people are on the wrong road, messing up life, they will continue to mess up unless they face the truth. If the only gift we give an abusive husband is compassion, then we are contributing to his evil. If we only try to understand a mean wife without speaking the truth to her, our love for her is incomplete. The gift of compassion must be accompanied by the gift of truth.

CHAPTER EIGHT

HONEST ANGER

A COMPASSIONATE
WARNING TO OTHERS

OBERTSON MCQUILKIN RESIGNED HIS JOB AS A university president to care for his wife, Muriel, who had Alzheimer's. It was not always easy.

Once, I completely lost it. In the days when Muriel could still stand and walk and we had not resorted to diapers, sometimes there were "accidents." I was on my knees beside her, trying to clean up the mess as she stood, confused by the toilet. It would have been easier if she weren't so insistent on helping. I got more and more frustrated. Suddenly, to make her stand still, I slapped her calf—as if that would do any good. It wasn't a hard slap, but she was startled. I was, too. Never in our 44 years of marriage had I ever so much touched her in anger or in rebuke of any kind. . . . Sobbing, I pled with her to forgive me—no matter that she didn't understand words any better than she could speak them. . . . It took me days to get over it. Maybe

God bottled those tears to quench the fires that might ignite again some day.[1]

Our sympathies are with Robertson. Sometimes we don't know what to do with our anger. All of a sudden, it's just there. It makes us feel uncomfortable, confused. Because of anger's volatility, some people avoid expressing it altogether. They deny that they are angry, only to have it come out in other ways, such as depression or irritability. Others vent their anger unchecked, regardless of the consequences. To them anger feels good, true, and righteous.

How did Jesus handle his anger? What angered him? What happened to his compassion when he was angry? Let's look at his interactions with the Pharisees to answer to these questions.

GOOD ANGER

The Jewish culture sets aside Saturday morning for worship. The synagogue in Capernaum is a large structure with a low ceiling, supported by columns.[2] As the guest speaker, Jesus would have begun by reading from the Law and the Prophets (the most important sections of the Jewish Scriptures). Then he would teach. But this particular morning is different.

> On another Sabbath Jesus went into the synagogue and was teaching, and a man was there whose right hand was shriveled. Looking for a reason to accuse Jesus, they watched him closely to see if he would heal on the Sabbath. They asked him, "Is it lawful to heal on the Sabbath?"
>
> Jesus said to the man with the shriveled hand, "Stand up in front of everyone."
>
> Then Jesus said to them, "If any of you has a sheep and it falls into a pit on the Sabbath, will you not take hold of it and lift it out? How much more valuable is a man than a sheep! Therefore it

is lawful to do good on the Sabbath." Then he asked them, "Which is lawful on the Sabbath: to do good or to do evil, to save life or to kill?" But they remained silent.

He looked around at them in anger. Deeply distressed at their stubborn hearts, Jesus said to the man, "Stretch out your hand." He stretched it out, and his hand was completely restored. Then the Pharisees went out and began to plot with the Herodians how they might kill Jesus.[3]

The leaders of the synagogue, sitting behind Jesus and facing the audience, ask Jesus a loaded question: *"Is it lawful to heal on the Sabbath?"* A man with a withered right hand is in the audience. Not only is this man unable to work, he has to endure the shame of not being a full member of Israel. As a disabled person, he's not permitted into the inner temple.

At other times when Jesus healed on the Sabbath, he healed first and then was criticized. Here the Pharisees initiate the discussion, suggesting that they planted the man with the withered hand in the audience. Again they are treating a person as an object. They use him to get Jesus into trouble.

Initially Jesus doesn't answer. He responds by having the man stand up in front of everyone so they can see him and his crippled hand. Then Jesus uses an example from daily life, connecting their care of sheep to this man. *"If any of you has a sheep and it falls into a pit on the Sabbath, will you not take hold of it and lift it out?"* Using the pattern of rabbinical argument, Jesus argues from the lesser to the greater: "If you'll take care of a sheep, won't you take care of this man?" Jesus wants to get them into this man's shoes by way of their sheep.

Earlier we saw Jesus incarnate with the weak. Here, he incarnates with the powerful, stepping into their shoes. He shows patience—compassion—to the Pharisees, even as he teaches them about compassion. He puts himself into their world, seeking to pull them out of their cold, religious legalism and into caring for this disabled man. Their own principles argued for doing good and saving lives. He concludes by asking them, *"Which is lawful on the Sabbath: to do good or to do evil, to save life or to kill?"* He turns the Pharisees' initial, judgmental question into a plea for mercy. It is a powerful sermon.

Unwilling to give Jesus permission to heal, the Pharisees are silent. Too locked into their manmade rules, they can't feel compassion. Their silence says that this man has less value than their sheep.

Enraged by their lack of compassion, Jesus scans the audience, looking for someone to approve the healing and relieve the man's suffering. No one moves. His anger wells up into saddened disgust at their callousness. He grieves at their heartlessness. But Jesus' anger and grief lead to an act of love. He commands the man to stretch out his shriveled hand, forcing everyone to look at it. Then, in front of their eyes, he heals the man. Jesus doesn't vent or "get things off his chest." He says little—and what he says and does is constructive. Love controls Jesus' expression of anger.

Not a mix of half-anger and half-compassion, Jesus is all compassion and all anger—a perfect expression of love for the victims of injustice. When we see someone suffer, we should feel compassion; when we see someone make another suffer, we should feel anger.

After Jesus heals the man, the Pharisees get so angry that they work on the Sabbath by plotting to kill him. Jesus has broken their personal rules and made them look bad. Their self-centered anger leads to retaliation rather than to love.

GOOD IRRITATION

People usually get irritated—the mildest form of anger—because things don't go their way. We tiptoe around irritable people. And we often justify our own irritation, because we are "hurt," yet we feel guilty because we've overreacted. So we talk about our "hurt" and try to forget our guilt.

But watch Jesus express his irritation with his disciples:

People were bringing little children to Jesus to have him touch them, but the disciples rebuked them. When Jesus saw this, he was indignant. He said to them, "Let the little children come to me, and do not hinder them, for the kingdom of God belongs to such as these. I tell you the truth, anyone who will not receive the kingdom of God like a little child will never enter it." And he took the children in his arms, put his hands on them and blessed them. (Mark 10:13-16)

Today, politicians love the publicity they get from kissing babies, but throughout most of history, people expected children to be seen and not heard. The disciples' rebuke to these parents reflected how society viewed children: Don't bother the important adults. But this attitude bothers Jesus, because the disciples are hindering the kind of people he's most interested in. In the Sermon on the Mount, he said: *"Blessed are the poor in spirit, for theirs is the kingdom of heaven. Blessed are the meek, for they will inherit the earth"* (Matthew 5:3,5).

According to Jesus, acknowledging our neediness opens the door to genuine and lasting happiness. Religions usually talk about what a person has to "do", but Jesus talks about what we "can't do". He says that our weakness, not our power or what we bring to God, enables us to know God. The "poor in spirit," those empty of their own sense of strength—that is, children—really understand this. The "meek," those who don't exercise power, are the real heroes, which is very good news, because most of us know we don't have it all together.

Jesus doesn't just see children as examples of powerlessness; he values them. He holds and touches them, and gets irritated when they get pushed aside. We become irritated when others interrupt us and mess up our attempts to look good or be efficient. Jesus becomes irritated when he can't be interrupted. He loves to love.

Irritation is not wrong, in and of itself. When other people do wrong things, we should get irritated. Our irritation, rightly used to act in love, can fuel a few honest words, which in turn can help people.

GOOD RAGE

Now let's look at Jesus when he is at his angriest. This incident took place just before Passover, a few days before Jesus' death:

> On reaching Jerusalem, Jesus entered the temple area and began driving out those who were buying and selling there. He overturned the tables of the money changers and the benches of those selling doves. . . . He said, "Is it not written: 'My house will be called a house of prayer for all nations'? But you have made it 'a den of robbers.'" (Mark 11:15,17)

One man, by the sheer force of his anger, kicks over tables, thundering in rage, "'My house will be called a house of prayer for all nations,' but you are making it 'a den of robbers.'" The commercialization of religion angers Jesus. The worship of God has been turned into the worship of money. The din of clanking change has replaced the sounds of heartfelt prayer. The kingdom of noise had replaced the kingdom of God.

Jews came from all over the Roman world and beyond to worship in the Jerusalem temple. When they changed their money in order to buy lambs for the sacrifice, the priests received kickbacks. This angered Jesus.

The Law of Moses prescribed that a lamb sacrificed in payment for sins had to be perfect, but the priests said that only their lambs were perfect—so the Jews had to purchase their lambs, giving the religious professionals a tidy profit, as monopolies usually do. This hurt the poor most of all, and it made Jesus angry.[4]

All of this commerce took place in the outer court of the temple, which was reserved for prayer by other ethnic groups (only Jews went into the inner courts). The ancient prophecies said that one

LOVE WALKED AMONG US

day the Jews would bring salvation to "all" people. Israel would be the door through which people from all nations would come to know God. But because the priests were using the outer court for commerce, the Gentiles couldn't use it to pray. (Imagine trying to watch a school play while someone is loudly hawking beer in the aisles.) This angered Jesus too.

His honest anger compassionately warns people of danger. Many scholars believe that Jesus was acting out a parable of judgment in the temple that foreshadowed the destruction of Jerusalem in A.D. 70 by the Roman general Titus—warning Israel that unless they change, the temple will be destroyed. It was an implicit claim to kingship because the great kings of Israel had ultimate authority over the temple. But for the Jewish leadership, Jesus' actions were the equivalent of burning an American flag in front of the capitol building.

In Jesus we see a person who loves and values children one minute and then flips tables the next. How do we put this together? C. S. Lewis portrays this side of Jesus in *The Lion, the Witch, and the Wardrobe*. Susan and Lucy are talking with Mr. and Mrs. Beaver about Aslan, a lion who symbolizes Jesus:

> "Is he—quite safe? I shall feel rather nervous about meeting a lion," said Lucy.
>
> "That you will dearie, and no mistake," said Mrs. Beaver, "if there's anyone who can appear before Aslan without his knees knocking, they're either braver than most or else just silly."
>
> "Then he isn't safe?" said Lucy.
>
> "Safe?" said Mr. Beaver. "Don't you hear what Mrs. Beaver tells you? Who said anything about safe? 'Course he isn't safe. But he's good. He's the King, I tell you."[5]

Both gentle and strong, humble and powerful, Jesus embodies the Tender Warrior.

JESUS, THE DISTURBER OF PEACE

We might have a few people in mind who need a good dose of Jesus' anger, but we'd rather not have it directed at us. Jesus' anger is uncomfortable. He is both the true-peacemaker and the false-peacebreaker. Jesus' angry honesty disrupts false peace.

In one of his private sessions with his disciples, Jesus says: *"Do not suppose that I have come to bring peace to the earth. I did not come to bring peace, but a sword"* (Matthew 10:34). Disturbing words, they are seldom quoted. Didn't Jesus also say, *"Blessed are the peacemakers"* (Matthew 5:9)? Isn't this a contradiction? If you think about evil and the need for justice, Jesus' comment makes perfect sense. Even though honesty can be painful and justice often separates, honesty and justice resolve injustice. Compassion without truth and justice is an ugly, spineless parody of love.

Jesus gets angry at callousness, arrogance, and injustice. Some things ought not to be. Abuse should be corrected. Think back on a time when you have seen or experienced evil. Imagine Jesus angrily confronting that situation: "This ought not to be." Justice satisfies. It restores sanity. It brings balance back to life. Some things are always wrong, sins against both God and other people. Deep down, we all know there is right and wrong, true and false.

One of my college professors gave us the assignment of creating our own ethical systems. I asked him, "What if I were a Nazi, and I wanted to create my own ethical code?" He didn't say anything. He was caught between a surface commitment to relativism (you can create your own moral system), and a deeply felt belief that murder is wrong (one of the Ten Commandments, God's moral code). I was not being flippant—I knew he was Jewish and both of us abhorred Nazism, yet I wanted him to face the logic of what

96

Mitya says in Dostoevsky's *Brothers Karamazov*: "If there's no God and no life beyond the grave, doesn't that mean that men will be allowed to do whatever they want?"[6]

My professor wanted to hang on to his relativism and yet condemn Hitler as absolutely wrong. Unwilling to admit his commitment to morality, he got angry with me. His anger was self-protective—he didn't like his hypocrisy exposed, his peace disturbed.

OTHER-CENTERED ANGER

It's a treat to see good anger because it's so rare. Remarkably, Jesus never gets angry when people hurt him—the very point where we might blow our stacks. Even on another occasion when the Pharisees call him demon-possessed, he responds matter-of-factly. Because he holds onto his time and schedule so lightly, he doesn't get irritated at being interrupted. Because he owns so little, he has little fuel for the fire. Yet he gets upset with injustice and hypocrisy in others when compassion is blocked. His anger is centered on others' welfare.

He also gets upset with anything that inhibits faith. The disciples blocked the faith of the little children. The money changers blocked the faith of the non-Jews. Jesus gets angry at anything that prevents love to people (compassion) or dependence on God (faith).

Jesus expresses his anger vividly, but it's always controlled. Only his eyes blaze when the leaders refuse to bless the healing of the crippled man. Even in the temple, he is focused specifically on the object of his wrath: the money changers. And his anger always does good—a man gets a new hand, children get hugged, money changers get ejected, and the temple gets quiet. His anger is powerful, controlled, and creative.

CHAPTER NINE

A TIME TO SHUT UP

BALANCING HONESTY
WITH COMPASSION

WALTER, A FRIEND OF MINE, CAME HOME EXCITED because a fellow worker had apologized to him for something he had done several years before. Walter told his wife, and she responded with a curt, "Oh, whatever." He was initially taken aback, stung by his wife's response. But after a few minutes, he asked her where she had purchased some new furniture and they talked about how it would best fit in the room.

When Walter mentioned this to me, I wondered why he didn't retaliate with silence when she dismissed him, in effect telling her: "You aren't interested in me, why should I be interested in you?" Why did he take an interest in her?

He told me that he had known his wife was still smarting from some honest words he said to her a couple days before. Why add another wound when the first one hadn't healed? He also knew she was having a hard time with someone else. It might have spilled over into her conversation with him. And he knew she wasn't feeling well. And there simply wasn't the time to be honest in a way that would be helpful. Walter's honesty was shaped by his compassion for his wife.

Walter reminds me of Jesus. Jesus' honest confrontation was always "for" people. He was for the weeping woman at Simon's house, but he was also for Simon, because it wasn't right for him to judge and mistreat people. Likewise Jesus was for Martha, because it wasn't right for her to lash out at her sister in jealousy. He kindly confronts the disciples when they callously judge the blind man. He patiently defends Mary, asserting that she had done a good thing.

A STUDY IN PATIENCE

At their last meal together, the Last Supper, Jesus warns the disciples that they will desert him when the going gets rough during his trial and execution. Peter, the disciple who later denied Jesus three times, insists that he will never desert Jesus.

> "You will all fall away," Jesus told them, "for it is written: 'I will strike the shepherd, and the sheep will be scattered. . . .'"
> Peter declared, "Even if all fall away, I will not."
> "I tell you the truth," Jesus answered, "today—yes, tonight— before the rooster crows twice you yourself will disown me three times."
> But Peter insisted emphatically, "Even if I have to die with you, I will never disown you." And all the others said the same.
> (Mark 14:27-31)

The Greek indicates that Peter "kept on insisting;" he didn't give it a rest, but Jesus lets Peter have the last word. He doesn't demand that Peter say, "Jesus, I understand what you're saying, and you've always been right about things, so I suspect you're right with this as well."

When someone rejects our honesty, we often repeat what we've said, only with more volume and more adverbs. We say, "You *never* listen. You *always* . . . " The last thing we want to do is just be quiet and listen or even comfort someone, but that is exactly what Jesus does. After Jesus told Peter about his denial, Jesus comforted the disciples: *"Do not let your hearts be troubled. Trust in God; trust also in me"* (*John 14:1*).

Jesus was honest "for" them. By telling them what would soon happen, he helped prepare them for the shock of his death and their desertion of him. He doesn't force the issue when they object. He just gives them space to mull it over, giving us a picture of honesty controlled by compassion.

RELEASING THE DEMAND FOR JUSTICE

Some people fear that if they don't tell other people "what they need to hear," they are being controlled by them. But the exact opposite is true. We don't need to express our thoughts every time we are hurt or people resist our honesty. We don't need to voice every concern or criticism. We don't always need to say what is on our mind. We can handle something purely internally.

Silently "shutting up," forgiving, often feels unfair, and that makes it difficult and painful enough. But in the first century, society viewed forgiveness as preposterous; they didn't even value it in theory.[1] All that counted was "saving face." You save face by exacting revenge for the slightest insult.

But Jesus advocates a different way, and shows us how to deal with the unfairness of forgiving someone who has wronged us. Once Peter asked him, *"Lord, how many times shall I forgive my brother when he sins against me? Up to seven times?"* Someone had likely irritated Peter; and he must have felt very good about his newfound spirituality, because the rabbis said that you had to forgive someone three times. But Jesus, unpredictable as always, tells Peter, *"I tell you, not seven times, but seventy-seven times"* (*Matthew 18:21-22*).

Jesus then explains forgiveness by telling a parable of a king's servant who owed his king ten thousand talents—an unheard-of amount of money, far too much to pay back. But when the servant begged for mercy, the king forgave him. Then the king's servant went to a fellow servant who owed him one hundred denarii— a serious debt, perhaps five thousand dollars, but a drop in the bucket compared to what he owed. The king's servant threw his fellow servant in prison until he could pay. The king got wind of this, became angry, and threw his servant in jail, saying, *"Shouldn't you have had mercy on your fellow servant just as I had on you?"* (*Matthew 18:33*).

Jesus ends the story with these words, *"This is how my heavenly Father will treat each of you unless you forgive your brother from your heart"* (*verse 35*). The implication is: "Peter, your honesty to someone who has wronged you needs to be tempered by seeing how much God has forgiven you for the wrongs you have done to him." When we see what we are really like from God's perspective, it has a way of shutting us up when we want to point the finger at others.

Honesty demands justice, but forgiveness releases the demand for justice. When we forgive, we see our own need for mercy . . . not justice.

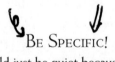

Be Specific!

Sometimes, we should just be quiet because our words aren't helpful. Statements such as "You just don't get it" or "You never listen" or "Can't you ever do anything right?" or "You are so emotional" are destructive, partly because they aren't specific about what the other person has done wrong. The words may contain some truth, but the sweeping generalizations make the messages judgmental and meaningless.

Watch how Jesus backs up his generalizations about the Pharisees with specific examples. When warning the crowds and his disciples about the Pharisees, he says:

"Everything they do is done for men to see: They make their phylacteries wide [little boxes that contained passages from the law of Moses] and the tassels on their garments long; they love the place of honor at banquets and the most important seats in the synagogues; they love to be greeted in the marketplaces and to have men call them 'Rabbi.'" (Matthew 23:5-7)

It takes time and thought to articulate exactly what a person is doing wrong, yet Jesus gives six specific examples of the Pharisees showing off, giving them a window through which to see themselves. He's incarnating again—slowing down, thinking about someone else's world, and thoughtfully speaking into that world.

Jesus told his disciples, *"If your brother sins against you, go and show him his fault, just between the two of you. If he listens to you, you have won your brother over"* (Matthew 18:15). How can we put this into practice? Let's say that, at times, your dad can be very critical. He is so confident of his wisdom that he frequently criticizes others and shows them his "better way." Honesty with someone like your dad is so hard that you either write him off or wait until he really irritates you, and then use your anger to jump-start your honesty with a sweeping statement like, "You are so arrogant." You blow his head off, but he has no idea what you mean and gets upset. You get angrier because he doesn't listen, and you walk away, never wanting to have anything to do with him again. You dump, then run. ~~that's bad...~~

Instead, wait for a specific time when your dad says something critical and say: "At dinner the other day when Mom was telling that story about the kids, I know she didn't get all the details straight, but you corrected her two or three times. You came across as being better than her. It just seemed unnecessary because I know how much you love her." Walk toward him with your thoughtful honesty.

Even Jesus' honesty, which involves making accurate judgments, reflects his summary of himself: *"I did not come to judge the world, but* to save it" (*John* 12:47). Even when he makes judgments, he is saving people.

But combining compassion and honesty is easier said than done. In the next chapter, we look at how Jesus does it

Two sides
_____

Nice Guy - won't be honest

"Righteous Guy" - honest but judgmental

Both leads to distancing of relationships.

We don't care enough

broken relationships are what cement a church we're like broken bones but Jesus Christ mends us and we're stronger.

LOVE WALKED AMONG US

CHAPTER TEN

"I KNOW HOW HARD IT IS; I DO THE SAME THING"

BEING HONEST WITHOUT BEING JUDGMENTAL

NE SATURDAY NIGHT, JILL AND I WENT DANCING with some good friends. We had taken a dance course the year before, and this was our first try at the real thing. Going to the ballroom was like traveling in a time warp back to the 1940s. I think we were the only ones there who weren't on Social Security.

Jill was having a great time just watching people. She could do it for hours. I was thinking, "We've taken dance lessons, we've traveled forty-five minutes to get here, so it is a waste of time not to dance." I didn't really want to pressure Jill, yet I kept bringing it up until she buckled. So we danced.

But we had a problem. Jill keeps a great beat, but didn't know the steps. I knew the steps, but couldn't keep a beat. "Fortunately," there is a rule in dancing that takes care of potential problems—the man is supposed to lead.

Within a minute or so, I got off beat and Jill corrected it by leading. I got irritated at her for leading, and she told me, "Now I know why I don't like to dance. You get angry."

So we sat down for a few minutes. Then we decided to give it another go by splitting up and dancing with our friends. We did that for a few minutes, got the steps and rhythm down, tried again, and it worked. We had a good time that evening, but we both felt tense. We needed reconciliation.

In the Sermon on the Mount Jesus says if you are in the temple, offering your sacrifice *"at the altar and there remember that your brother has something against you, leave your gift there in front of the altar. First go and be reconciled to your brother; then come and offer your gift"* (Matthew 5:23-24). In other words, don't bother worshiping God if you aren't reconciled in your relationships. Loving people is more important than formal religion. If there is a kink in a relationship, drop everything and go fix it. Initiate discussion—even if the problem is the other's fault. Love always moves toward people to restore relationships.

Using Beam Research

At the end of the evening of dancing, Jill and I were both irritated at each other. We both thought the other person needed to listen and change. I felt Jill was ninety percent at fault, and she thought I was ninety percent at fault. How could we reconcile and yet be honest with each other?

In the Sermon on the Mount, Jesus imagines a scenario where we want to give someone "a piece of our mind." He challenges us:

> *"Why do you look at the speck of sawdust in your brother's eye and pay no attention to the beam in your own eye? How can you say to your brother, 'Let me take the speck out of your eye,' when all the time there is a beam in your own eye? You hypocrite, first take the beam out of your own eye, and then you will see clearly to remove the speck from your brother's eye."* (Matthew 7:3-5)[1]

LOVE WALKED AMONG US

This illustration implies a peculiar twist to the human heart: the failings that bother us in others mirror our own failings. We judge others for their failings (*specks of sawdust*) even as we overlook our own considerably larger ones (*beams*). Try Jesus' insight on yourself. What bugs you about other people? Do you, in some way, do the same thing? For instance, does it bother you when you see someone insensitive to women? Have you ever been uncaring toward a woman? If you follow Jesus' teaching, your attitude won't be, "How can you be so stupid?" but, "I know how hard it is. I do the same thing." Jesus says we should examine ourselves and remove our own flaws before pointing out someone else's.

He wants us to see that our inner evil affects our eyesight. Our self-righteousness, our sense that "we would never do that," distorts our vision so that the other person's errors loom larger than our own. So when the person doesn't listen, we just increase the volume. Honesty becomes a weapon. If you and I are both doing this, we enter a self-defeating cycle of blaming and defending. But if I focus first on myself, I break the cycle and make peace possible. Then I'm not above you, telling you to come up to my level. I'll be asking you to join me as a person who needs mercy and help. Compassion begins by looking at the other person. Reconciliation begins by looking at yourself.

The Golden Rule tells us to reflect first on ourselves and how we'd like someone to love us, then to use that information to love a friend. Beam Research says to first reflect on how we do similar things, and then use that information to be honest with our friend. When we own up to our own problems first, our holier-than-thou attitude disappears, leaving only a compassionate honesty.

Jesus taught others to do Beam Research, but we never see him do any. He never reflects on his own sin. Why? He gives us a clue when he asks the Pharisees, *"Can any of you prove me guilty of sin?"* (*John* 8:46). This claim to be sinless makes sense if Jesus is God-in-the-flesh. We'd expect God to be sinless, and therefore unable to do Beam Research.

"You Who Are Without Sin ..."

In the following scene Jesus again underscores our need for Beam Research:

> At dawn he appeared again in the temple courts, where all the people gathered around him, and he sat down to teach them. The teachers of the law and the Pharisees brought in a woman caught in adultery. They made her stand before the group and said to Jesus, "Teacher, this woman was caught in the act of adultery. In the Law Moses commanded us to stone such women. Now what do you say?" They were using this question as a trap, in order to have a basis for accusing him.
>
> But Jesus bent down and started to write on the ground with his finger. When they kept on questioning him, he straightened up and said to them, "If any one of you is without sin, let him be the first to throw a stone at her." Again he stooped down and wrote on the ground.
>
> At this, those who heard began to go away one at a time, the older ones first, until only Jesus was left, with the woman standing there. Jesus straightened up and asked her, "Woman, where are they? Has no one condemned you?"
>
> "No one, sir," she said.
>
> "Then neither do I condemn you," Jesus declared. "Go now and leave your life of sin." (John 8:2-11)

The Pharisees have laid a trap. If Jesus doesn't condemn the woman, they have caught him in a violation of the Law of Moses, and he is not a good Jew. But if Jesus condemns this woman, he violates his reputation for compassion and puts himself in conflict with the Romans (who forbid the Jews to carry out the death penalty).

In response to the trap, Jesus bends down and silently begins to write on the ground with his finger. After they persist, he looks up and gives the men permission to stone the woman, if they first declare they are without sin. Then he resumes writing on the ground. Jesus gives them space and time so his words can pierce their hearts. He wants them to judge their own hearts first in order to let the air out of their self-righteousness. The only way to be honest without being judgmental is not by learning a principle, but by going through a process where you reflect, How do I do the same thing?

Slowly, one by one, the accusers walk away. As they began to do Beam Research, they were convicted that their words and their lives didn't match. Likely they were convicted of their own adultery, either physical or mental. (Jesus says, ". . . *anyone who looks at a woman lustfully has already committed adultery with her in his heart*" [*Matthew* 5:28].)

Possibly, they were convicted of a double standard when it came to women and men. It takes two to tango, but the guy is not there. Furthermore, in order to be caught in adultery, the Mosaic Law said that at least two witnesses had to catch a person in the act of intercourse. The husband was forbidden by law to entrap his wife by waiting for her in hiding; yet it's likely that's what happened here, because the Pharisees had to find a woman who had committed adultery in order to trap Jesus. Whatever the case, Jesus' question exposed their failure to live up to their own rules.[2] The more they thought, the heavier the rocks around the woman began to look.

Jesus simplifies a complex situation by encouraging self-reflective repentance. He did not simplify the situation, as our culture does, by saying that adultery is okay because it feels good. He affirms God's rule *"You shall not commit adultery"* when he tells her *"sin no more."* The law itself was not corrupt—the corruption was in the accusers' hearts, in their self-righteousness.

LEARNING TO DANCE

Clearly, Beam Research is painful. As I reflected on the tension between Jill and me, I dreaded talking with her. I would have to draw out from her something about me that I didn't want to hear, and that she didn't want to share because at times I had rejected her honesty.

The next morning I asked Jill how I had hurt her the previous evening. She said, "Why did we even have to dance? Couldn't we have just sat there and watched the people?" She pointed to my pushiness and anger. That evening I asked her again how I had affected her the previous evening. She talked about the other couple: "Did you see how our friends loved one another? Did you see how he tilted his head toward her because he delighted in her? How he concentrates, looks at her? You don't love me that way."

I was stunned. That day I began to love Jill in ways I never had before. When she took the risk of opening up her heart to me, I began to understand what it was to cherish someone, to love the way Jesus does—by being attentive, strong, tender, powerful, constant, enduring, and self-forgetting.

Later that day I told Jill it would have been easier for me if she had told me that I was off-beat when we were dancing, rather than just starting to lead. When I told her this, she got angry. I asked her why it was okay for her to be honest but not me, and she began to listen quietly.

Jesus' prescription for a gentle honesty—*"first take the beam out of your eye, and then you will see clearly to take the speck out of your brother's eye"*—guided my love for Jill. Only after asking Jill questions for a full day did I *see clearly*. By the time I finished doing Beam Research, my own wound had gotten smaller because I saw my own wrong-doing. Then instead of a self-righteous lecture, my honesty became a quiet, one-sentence question.

A Word of Caution

But what do we do when, no matter how much we try to change, the other person doesn't receive honesty from us? How can we be honest with someone when everything we say is interpreted through a negative grid, when kindness is construed as manipulation and used against us?

Jesus speaks to this in a pithy parable after the teaching on the speck and beam: *"Do not give dogs what is sacred; do not throw your pearls to pigs. If you do, they may trample them under their feet, and then turn and tear you to pieces"* (Matthew 7:6).

Here's a rough interpretation of the parable: Some people (*pigs*) just can't handle honesty (*pearls*) from you, no matter how gentle, humble, or cautious you are. Even if you *take your beam out,* other people may not listen. In fact they will even misinterpret your compassion *and tear you to pieces.*

Jesus calls such a person an "enemy," someone who is against you. No matter what you do or say, enemies dislike you, read into your actions, and judge you; so if your words aren't accomplishing anything, be quiet. Such caution saves you from beating your head against the wall, trying to change a stubborn person.

Calling someone an enemy seems harsh or judgmental. We don't like to think of our spouse, child, or friend as an enemy, so we rush in with more words and try to fix the situation—only to make it worse. But the word "enemy" can be simply a temporary category to describe how someone is treating us. We are just observing, "this morning, my teenager is acting like an enemy." Sometimes with some people, more words make it worse. Reconciliation is the rule; silence with enemies is the exception to the rule.

Jesus told his disciples: *"Be as shrewd as snakes and as innocent as doves. Be on your guard against men"* (Matthew 10:16-17). Because our world is beautiful but broken, Jesus is loving yet wary. For example, when he spoke out against men who divorce their wives just because they want to "upgrade," he was speaking to the disciples privately, indoors (Mark 10:10). Why? Jesus' cousin, John the Baptist, was killed by Herod Agrippa for publicly denouncing Herod's divorce.[3] Jesus was even cautious with his followers: *"But*

Jesus would not entrust himself to them, for he knew all men. He did not need man's testimony about man, for he knew what was in a man" (John 2:24-25).

But be careful of going to the opposite extreme and calling people enemies just because they were mean to you—thus, avoiding the hard work of reconciliation. I've heard people say, "Oh, he would never listen," but they hadn't even tried. It was easier to decide ahead of time that the person wouldn't listen, and thus dismiss him as an "enemy."

How Do You Love an Enemy?

If we have followed Jesus' instructions for reconciliation and the person refuses to reconcile, what do we do? True to form, Jesus' advice goes against every instinct we have when someone hurts us. He tells us to love our enemies, to actively seek their good, and to care for the people we can't stand.

Jesus shows us how to love our enemies, taking examples from everyday life:

> *"You have heard that it was said, 'Eye for eye, and tooth for tooth.' But I tell you, Do not resist an evil person. If someone strikes you on the right cheek, turn to him the other also. And if someone wants to sue you and take your tunic, let him have your cloak as well. If someone forces you to go one mile, go with him two miles."* (Matthew 5:38-41)

Moses was the first to say, *eye for eye, and tooth for tooth.* This was not a prescription for revenge, but for curbing our natural reactions. Instinctively, we take two eyes for one, two teeth for one. We don't want equal justice; we want to punish, to extract more from them than they took from us. Here Jesus raises the bar of love to extraordinary heights, commanding not only that we love enemies, but also that we actively seek their good. Lest we miss the point,

LOVE WALKED AMONG US

he mentions the legal right of a Roman soldier to force a person to take his pack one mile. Not only are we to take the pack, we are to offer to take it a second mile. Instead of exacting twice the revenge, we are to give twice the love.

We don't stop loving difficult people; we just love them differently—without words. Switch to deeds, give the person a little space, and wait for God to work. He can put together what we can't.

To explain this characteristic of love, Jesus points to God, who gives indiscriminately. He says:

> *"You have heard that it was said, 'Love your neighbor and hate your enemy.' But I tell you: Love your enemies and pray for those who persecute you, that you may be sons of your Father in heaven. He causes his sun to rise on the evil and the good, and sends rain on the righteous and the unrighteous." (Matthew 5:43-45)*

Jesus practiced what he preached here. He even loved the people who killed him. When the soldiers are nailing him to the cross, Jesus actively seeks the welfare of the Roman soldiers by erasing their debt through forgiveness. He says, *"Father, forgive them, for they do not know what they are doing"* (Luke 23:34). The Greek indicates that Jesus *kept on saying*, *"Father, forgive them."*

BITTERNESS DIES, PEACE ENSUES

Is Jesus a masochist? That kind of love sounds crazy. Won't we open ourselves up for more hurt? No. Think about it. There are two problems with enemies. What they did hurts, and as we obsess about what they did, bitterness sets in like a claw in the brain. We become so focused on the hurt that we don't notice the bitterness slowly eating away at us—like cancer of the soul. Bitterness quietly transforms us so we become just like our enemy.

Jesus' command to love your enemies takes the energy out of bitterness. Instead of plotting revenge, we plan how to do them good. We reflect on their needs and how to help. The Roman soldier is tired, so we offer to take the pack a second mile. We love him where he's weak. Love like this takes our own heart by surprise and healing begins. Bitterness dies for lack of fuel.

Love also breaks the cycle of evil, keeping us from becoming like the enemy. Instead we become like Jesus—(free)—no longer controlled by the other person's evil. What's more, love unnerves an enemy, throwing him off guard. But best of all, it makes room for God's justice and mercy. To love an enemy means to trust that God is far more effective than I am. It takes faith to love.

During World War II Gandhi ceased confronting the British, his enemy, and supported their war effort, actively seeking their good. The result? Only a few years later, British opposition to India's independence collapsed. Love was too powerful.

Jesus' teaching to *"love your enemies"* reflects the ancient Jewish prophecy that the Messiah would be a *"Prince of Peace"* (Isaiah 9:6-7). It also fleshes out his words, *"Blessed, are the peacemakers."* By loving our enemies, by taking the beam out of our own eye, we become a peacemaker.

If I met someone exactly like me, I would not like that person because we know the flaws of ourselves. That's how judgmental we are but it's by the grace of God that other people can love us.

2-18-13

Andrew,
Flaws or no flaws, you're still an awesome fella! I'm really glad that God allowed our paths to cross at good ol' Shenandoah. Thanks for being interested in among people + for loving to talk to Jesus. God loves you yesterday, today + always!
Amy

PART 3

LOVE
DEPENDS
ON GOD

CHAPTER ELEVEN

THE SECRET TO LOVE

DEPENDENCE ON GOD

ART OF MY WORK IS TEACHING WEEKEND seminars. I begin one of my favorite lessons by writing on a flip chart, "I do nothing on my own. I can only do what I see my dad doing." I ask people to analyze the person who said this based only on this scrap of information. They quickly warm to the task and become instant, armchair psychologists:

"He sounds weak. Almost helpless."

"Does he have a mind of his own?"

"If he's an adult, he needs a little separation from his dad."

"Has this person been to counseling?"

"Not healthy."

"Very childlike."

"He's codependent."

After I've let the hook go deep, I tell them that Jesus said those words. *"I tell you the truth, the Son can do nothing by himself; he can do only what he sees his Father doing, because whatever the Father does, the Son also does. . . . By myself I can do nothing"* (John 5:19,30).

We see this kind of dependence as unhealthy. Americans in particular prize independence and trusting themselves, but at the foundation of Jesus' life lies a childlike trust in God, whom he calls "Father." Jesus is not controlled by a rulebook but by a relationship, so the choices he makes—when to be compassionate and when to be honest—come from God.

Controlled by God

Notice Jesus' dependence on his heavenly Father when his brothers suggest a change in his schedule:

> But when the Jewish Feast of Tabernacles was near, Jesus' brothers said to him, "You ought to leave here and go to Judea, so that your disciples may see the miracles you do. No one who wants to become a public figure acts in secret. Since you are doing these things, show yourself to the world." For even his own brothers did not believe in him.
>
> Therefore Jesus told them, "The right time for me has not yet come; for you any time is right. . . . You go to the Feast. I am not yet going up to this Feast, because for me the right time has not yet come." Having said this, he stayed in Galilee. (John 7:2-6, 8-9)

Jesus tells his brothers, "for you any time is right," implying that they are free to do what they want, when they want. But of himself, he says, "the right time for me has not yet come." His agenda is shaped by his Father; even details such as when he should go up to the Feast of Tabernacles.

His brothers are giving Jesus a lesson in marketing: "If you want to become famous, you must get your name out there." When the Jews celebrated the Feast of Tabernacles, the population of Jerusalem swelled to over a million. His family assumes that, like them, Jesus loves the cheers of the crowd. As an up-and-coming politician, Jesus needs their help to craft his image. And, of course, he will remember his family when he becomes a power broker.

But Jesus doesn't care about fame or power, only the will of his Father, so he tells them "no." Note that although the brothers appear free they are really bound by people's opinions, while Jesus' submission to God's will frees him from people's opinions.

The brothers want Jesus to do miracles at the Feast that millions will see, and in turn, make Jesus famous and powerful. But Jesus knows that these miracles would not be acts of love but manipulations for power. Such selfish motivations would pollute love like a skunk in the basement during a party. No matter how much we open the upstairs windows, no matter how much we perfume the house, if we mix selfishness with love, the smell keeps floating up, infecting everything.

Jesus' brothers would have interpreted his freedom as self-will because in the first century you just didn't think and act outside of your extended family of brothers, cousins, aunts, and uncles.

But Jesus has a different center of gravity: *"I do not accept praise from men, but I know you. I know that you do not have the love of God in your hearts. . . . How can you believe if you accept praise from one another, yet make no effort to obtain the praise that comes from the only God?"* (John 5:41-42,44). Because Jesus *"has the love of God in his heart,"* he doesn't need love from other sources. His bondage to his Father frees him to say "no" to his brothers and "yes" to people in pain. Without his underlying submission to God, Jesus would be trapped by other people's agendas and his own culture. He would be hurrying off to Jerusalem with his brothers, partly trying to keep his family happy, partly trying to become famous.

We are now down in the basement of love. Compassion and honesty, the visible first and second floors of love, rest on the foundation of dependence on God. We simply cannot love on our own. We need reference to another will (God's will) for direction and wisdom. Dependence on God means surrendering my will to his. It means saying to God, "You're the boss."

Saying "Yes" to Self Pollutes Our Love

We're using a new method of speech therapy with Kim that works on the muscle tone in her mouth so that she can learn to breathe consistently and sustain speech. She's learning how to blow in slow, steady breaths. One particular morning Kim was being very difficult, absolutely refusing to even try. I was feeling sorry for "poor Kim" and wondered if something was wrong, but Jill thought Kim was just being stubborn. We discussed this over breakfast, and overhearing us, Kim typed, "Stop arguing. I am the boss."

Our daughter Ashley and her husband, Dave, had Kim over for the weekend not long ago. By the end of the weekend, Dave was in shock: "Wow, is she stubborn! She even uses her disabilities to get her way." Kim is not alone. Willfulness—wanting our own way—can be so strong and yet so subtle, polluting our love.

Let's explore this with an interaction between a husband and a wife. The husband takes out the trash each week, but he forgot to do it last week, and he forgot again this week. Usually, he's good about taking out the trash, but the wife tells him, "Honey, you forgot to take out the trash again." The word "again" is a skunk in the basement, the not-so-subtle reminder that the husband is a failure. By pointing to his failure, the wife subtly enhances her own goodness. If we don't have *the love of God in our heart,* then we need to steal love from other sources. The word "again" steals a small cookie of love.

But she tells herself, "If I don't say "again," then he'll keep forgetting. If I don't show him this is becoming a pattern, I'll be doing the trash regularly." Notice the underlying assumption: "It all depends on me. If I don't show him, no one else will." God is completely absent from her thinking. In the absence of God's active intervention, she believes her husband "must" hear her words; otherwise it feels like she will be swallowed up by her husband's forgetfulness. She speaks on her own, using the word "again" to control her husband. But Jesus said, *"For I did not speak of my own accord, but the Father who sent me commanded me what to say and how to say it"* (John 12:49).

So how could the wife have been honest, yet not self-willed, in this situation? She could start by dropping the word "again," and then she could do some Beam Research—first asking herself if she had forgotten something twice lately. Or she could quietly take out the trash on her own, without saying anything. Love quietly forbears. It does not keep a record of wrongs.

Saying "Yes" to God Frees Us to Love

When we say "no" to self and "yes" to God, our love is pure.

One day when Kim was about ten, she was reading upstairs in her room. She came down to the kitchen where I was sitting, and indicated she wanted help carrying an enormous stack of her Richard Scarry books to our makeshift den in the basement. She went down the steps ahead of me, holding her box of crayons, sliding on her bottom from one step to the next. About two-thirds of the way down, she stopped—she had spilled the crayons all over the steps.

Normally, I would put the books down and help her. But instead of immediately going to her aid, I asked, "Kim, do you want me to help you?" To my surprise, she shook her head. I wasn't sure what to do, so I stood on the steps and waited while she slowly picked up the crayons. It was only a couple of minutes, but it seemed like an hour. It occurred to me that because it was hard for Kim to use her fingers, it was better for her to learn how to pick things up by herself. How quick I am to do obvious things when they might not be the best things.

Helping people can be tricky. It would look like I was doing something for Kim by picking up the crayons. But am I helping her, or am I just helping myself so I can get on to the next thing? In my study of Jesus, I've learned that love is not efficient. My wants, if gone unchecked, would have hurt Kim ever so slightly. By saying "no" to myself, my love for her could be pure, unpolluted by my own desires. Jesus commends the person who relates this way: *"Blessed are the meek"* (Matthew 5:5). Blessed are those who don't push their will on others.

A Hunger for Conversation with God

As I waited on the steps for Kim, I felt empty and disconcerted. This is often true when I stop doing what "I" want in a situation. When I disrupt my old ways of doing things, I often feel disoriented. But I also felt a quiet hunger to know God. When I stop doing my own will and the "me" dies, I start asking God what to do. I begin to live without "my agenda," and I become hungry for God.

We often see this in Jesus' life. In spite of his busyness, he was devoted to prayer: *Yet the news about him spread all the more, so that crowds of people came to hear him and to be healed of their sicknesses. But Jesus often withdrew to lonely places and prayed* (Luke 5:15-16). Prayer simply means "to ask." Through prayer, we ask God what we should do. Jesus teaches his disciples to pray by saying, *"Our Father in heaven . . . your will be done"* (Matthew 6:9-10). In prayer we surrender our will to God. Prayer doesn't exist in some mumbo-jumbo religious lingo—in prayer we have a personal conversation with the Creator. Prayer gives us direction about how to love. Without God's help, we are lost in a fog.

When Robertson McQuilkin left the university to take care of his wife, Muriel, a student asked him, "Do you miss being president?" As he reflected on the student's question, he put his wondering into a prayer:

> "Father, I like this assignment, and I have no regrets. But if a coach puts a man on the bench, he must not want him in the game. You needn't tell me, of course, but I'd like to know—why didn't you need me in the game?"
>
> I didn't sleep well that night and awoke contemplating

the puzzle. Muriel was still mobile at that time, so we set out on our morning walk around the block. She wasn't too sure on her feet, so we went slowly and held hands as we always do. This day I heard footsteps behind me and looked back to see the familiar form of a local derelict behind us. He staggered past us, then turned and looked us up and down. "Tha's good. I likes 'at," he said. "Tha's real good. I likes it." He turned and headed back down the street, mumbling to himself over and over again, "Tha's good. I like it."

When Muriel and I reached our little garden and sat down, his words came back to me. Then the realization hit me; God had spoken through an inebriated old derelict. "It is *you* who are whispering to my spirit, 'I likes it, tha's good,'" I said aloud. "I may be on the bench, but if you like it and say it's good, that's all that counts."[1]

When McQuilkin "heard" God's voice, he could "rest" in God's assignment for him. It deepened the meaning of his love for Muriel. Many times people give up on love because they get sick of hearing other people's voices — their demands. Then they walk away from a relationship and experience an initial freedom in regaining their own "voice." But our own voice can be just as tyrannical as someone else's voice. If we are in a walking, talking, dependent relationship with God, constantly hearing his voice, then we won't be caught between our own or other people's voices.

Prayer also brings God into our stories. The wife with the trash-forgetting husband can ask God that her husband would remember the trash. Such a simple prayer request seems strange, but not if God really shapes things. She can also ask God to help her not throttle her husband with her words. Then the trash becomes part of the story of what God is doing in her and in her husband. Will she end up taking the trash out the rest of her life? Possibly. But

THE SECRET TO LOVE

when I've gotten into taking-out-the-trash-for-the-rest-of-my-life situations, I often find God present in a peculiar way. I discover God in the trash.

A Hunger for Words from God

Jesus' dependence on his Father involves listening to him as well as talking. Jesus lived, breathed, and taught Scripture. His Golden Rule is just a quote from the book of *Leviticus* (19:18), *"Love your neighbor as yourself."* His Beatitudes are mostly quotes from the Psalms.

To Jesus, Scripture meant more than a means of knowing his Father's will—it meant life. As he is dying on the cross, Jesus quotes a psalm to express his grief: *About the ninth hour Jesus cried out in a loud voice, "My God, my God, why have you forsaken me?"* (Matthew 27:46, from Psalm 22:1). In death people cling to what they value in life.

Jesus also claims scriptural authority when he commands his disciples to love: *"A new commandment I give you: Love one another"* (John 13:34). He speaks like a king: *the crowds were amazed at his teaching, because he taught as one who had authority* (Matthew 7:28-29). At the end of his life, Jesus refers to the unique power of his words: *"Heaven and earth will pass away, but my words will never pass away"* (Matthew 24:35). That is an astounding claim for a first-century Jewish peasant. But it's true. His words have not passed away— they've shaped Western civilization. The Bible is the all-time best seller and the annual best seller.

Some think that we have moved beyond a primitive belief in sacred writings, but most of us have some kind of Scripture or guide that we follow. In the confusion of life, people look for a "word" of authority, for information that will bring clarity and direction to our lives. Some watch the news, read the newspaper, or check their horoscopes. University professors refer to "the literature" (current thinking in a particular area) almost with reverence. Psychologists look to Freud. Revolutionaries look to Marx. Millions of Americans

LOVE WALKED AMONG US

look to Oprah. We search for a word that will order the chaos of life, a word that will make sense of the brokenness.

Each of us is shaped by a script, whether it is a book, a movie, or a therapist. The search for words of certainty is so pervasive that one suspects it is preprogrammed. Einstein reflected that "Human beings . . . dance to a mysterious tune, intoned in the distance by an invisible player."[2] Jesus danced to the words of what we call the Bible, which is a living letter from his heavenly Father. The words of Scripture shaped his life.

Words from the Bible were shaping me when I stopped on the steps and asked Kim if she wanted help. I had been thinking about how Jesus surrendered his will to God and how quick I was to do my own will. Usually, my will just felt like a really good idea, so it was hard to see. But written words from God were affecting me, slowing me down. If other family members had helped Kim, I wouldn't have thought twice about their actions. There was something very personal going on between me and God that came out of an ongoing communication that was connected to both prayer and the written Word.

Jesus interpreted life through the lens of his Father. He didn't say we should love our enemies because "that's what love does," he said we should love because that's what his Father is like. *"He . . . sends rain on the righteous and unrighteous"* (Matthew 5:45). And because the Father defines love, it is safe not to do my own will, not to follow the impulse of my good ideas, and to wait quietly for Kim on the steps. I didn't have to be efficient, because God is a loving Father orchestrating the details of my life—even spilled crayons.

Chapter Twelve

SAYING "NO" TO SOMEONE YOU LOVE

Compassionately Responding to Demands

*T*HE MOST STRIDENT VOICES IN OUR LIVES OFTEN come from our closest relationships—mothers, fathers, husbands, wives, children. They know us best and can use that knowledge to organize our lives. Sometimes, lurking behind their requests is a demand that we make their world trouble-free. How do we say "no" to someone we love? How do we say "no" without feeling guilty? How do we say "no," yet do them good at the same time? It seems easier to simply retaliate, withdraw, or offer the silent treatment. ←

Jesus' relationship with his mother gives us an example of how to compassionately respond to the demands of those we love. It is a study of saying "no."

In the early chapters of Luke's gospel, we see Mary as a young Jewish woman (probably about fourteen or fifteen) who quickly obeys God with a childlike, pristine faith. But as we read further in the Gospels, a richer, more human picture of Mary emerges.

Jesus Says "No" to Blame Shifting

When Jesus was about twelve years old, he went on a trip to Jerusalem with Mary and Joseph.

> *Every year his parents went to Jerusalem for the Feast of the Passover. When he was twelve years old, they went up to the Feast, according to the custom. After the Feast was over, while his parents were returning home, the boy Jesus stayed behind in Jerusalem, but they were unaware of it. Thinking he was in their company, they traveled on for a day. Then they began looking for him among their relatives and friends. When they did not find him, they went back to Jerusalem to look for him. After three days they found him in the temple courts, sitting among the teachers, listening to them and asking them questions. Everyone who heard him was amazed at his understanding and his answers. When his parents saw him, they were astonished. His mother said to him, "Son, why have you treated us like this? Your father and I have been anxiously searching for you."*
>
> *"Why were you searching for me?" he asked. "Didn't you know I had to be in my Father's house?" But they did not understand what he was saying to them.*
>
> *Then he went down to Nazareth with them and was obedient to them. But his mother treasured all these things in her heart. And Jesus grew in wisdom and stature, and in favor with God and men.* (Luke 2:41-52)

After looking for her son for three days among thousands of people, Mary feels tense and afraid, as any parent would. When she finds him, she blames Jesus for their separation and her worries. Unintimidated by her blame shifting, Jesus tells her she shouldn't have worried about him, that she should have known he'd be in the temple, his Father's house. Jesus simply expresses his desire to be with his heavenly Father. He feels no guilt or defensiveness, he simply goes back home with his parents and "obeys" them, as his Father had instructed: *"Honor your father and your mother"* (*Exodus* 20:12). He has a healthy independence from his parents, one that doesn't lead to rebellion. He says "no" to blame shifting but "yes" to going home with his parents. Jesus' love is not unconditional. It is conditioned and shaped by his Father.

We often fear submitting to others because we're afraid to lose control; we might have to do something we don't want to do. But if we are confident of God's control of people—whether parents or employers or anyone else in our life—then we can freely submit to that person's authority. Because we know that someone more powerful controls them, we can surrender. For example, suppose you have a difficult boss who loads you down with meaningless tasks. You can be patient with him if your dad is the CEO and has assured you that you won't suffer under him much longer.

Jesus Says "No" to Showing Off

Jesus' relationship with his Father also enables him to say "no" when his mother wants to show him off at a wedding they're attending. It's at the very beginning of his public ministry, and he has yet to perform any miracles.

> *On the third day a wedding took place in Cana in Galilee. Jesus' mother was there, and Jesus and his disciples had also been invited to the wedding. When the wine was gone, Jesus' mother said to him, "They have no more wine."*
>
> *"Dear woman, why do you involve me?" Jesus replied, "My time has not yet come."*
>
> *His mother said to the servants, "Do whatever he tells you."*
>
> *Nearby stood six stone water jars, the kind used by the Jews for ceremonial washing, each holding from twenty to thirty gallons. Jesus said to the servants, "Fill the jars with water"; so*

129

they filled them to the brim. Then he told them, "Now draw some out and take it to the master of the banquet."

They did so, and the master of the banquet tasted the water that had been turned into wine. He did not realize where it had come from, though the servants who had drawn the water knew. Then he called the bridegroom aside and said, "Everyone brings out the choice wine first and then the cheaper wine after the guests have had too much to drink; but you have saved the best till now." This, the first of his miraculous signs, Jesus performed at Cana in Galilee. He thus revealed his glory, and his disciples put their faith in him.
(John 2:1-11)

Cana is about seven miles north of Nazareth. Wedding feasts were week-long affairs during which the wedding guests were fed daily. To run out of wine was a major catastrophe—like forgetting the wedding cake. Mary learns of the wine shortage, and wants Jesus to do something about it. She doesn't accept Jesus' "no" (*"Dear woman why do you involve me?"*) for an answer, and tells the servants to get ready for him. She likely wants her fabulous son to "show his stuff." What mother doesn't want her son to look good?

When Jesus tells her, *"My time has not yet come,"* he's again saying he's submitting to God's timing, not someone else's—not even his mother's. (*My time* refers to Jesus' hour of glory, the moment in the spotlight when people see all the best that Jesus is.)

Jesus didn't have a problem with "what" Mary wanted (wine for the feast)—just "why" she wanted it (to show him off). "Why" Jesus does something is as important as "what" he does. Since he's secure with his Father, he doesn't have to prove his independence from Mary. So he agrees to take care of the wine shortage.

Though Jesus appears to be under Mary's thumb, he is so unselfconsciously humble that he does exactly what she

LOVE WALKED AMONG US

wants—unlike a husband who resists his wife's requests because he fears appearing subservient. But rather than a spectacular display that makes Jesus famous, the miracle is an act of love, done quietly to maintain the dignity of the young couple and their family. (They would have been shamed by a public display.) Jesus makes them appear very generous by making 150 gallons of fine wine—far more than they'll need. Because Jesus is at the party, it not only keeps going, it also gets better! God saved the best till last.

Jesus Says "No" to Family Pressure

Jesus soon begins to do miracles that relieve people's pain, hunger, sickness, and disabilities. Not surprisingly, thousands of people swamp him and his disciples.

> *Then Jesus entered a house, and again a crowd gathered, so that he and his disciples were not even able to eat. When his family heard about this, they went to take charge of him, for they said, "He is out of his mind." And the teachers of the law who came down from Jerusalem said, "He is possessed by Beelzebub! By the prince of demons he is driving out demons."*
>
> *So Jesus called them and spoke to them in parables: "How can Satan drive out Satan? If a kingdom is divided against itself, that kingdom cannot stand. But if I drive out demons by the Spirit of God, then the kingdom of God has come upon you."*
>
> *Then Jesus' mother and brothers arrived. Standing outside, they sent someone in to call him. A crowd was sitting around him, and they told him, "Your mother and brothers are outside looking for you." Then he looked at those seated in a circle around him and said, "Here are my mother and my brothers! Whoever does God's will is my brother and sister and mother."* (Mark 3:20-24, 31-35; Matthew 12:28)

Jesus' family thinks he has gone out of his mind. Such family intervention may seem odd today. If we thought a grown brother was in trouble or in over his head, we may speak with him, but we'd not likely come to take charge of him. But Jesus' family's concern for him was rooted in the shame/honor culture of the ancient Mediterranean world, which valued the group more than the individual. The individual draws his honor from the group, and likewise, has the potential of dishonoring his group or family. How Jesus fares reflects on his family as a whole. Thus, the family's actions stem partly from self-interest.[1] But if Jesus had permitted them to take control of him, he would have given into their agenda for the sake of family peace. When we agree with people just to shut them up, it looks like we're being nice when we are actually manipulating them.

Jesus rebuffs his family by referring to a higher standard than family, and to a different kind of family, a new community where *"whoever does God's will is my brother, sister, and mother."* Again we see Jesus' relationship with his Father defining his love, shaping his purpose. This anchor frees him from the guilt of "I should be doing more." Dependence on God, thus understood, protects us from others' restless demands and our own.

Jesus' family tries to control him, to force him to do their will because they think he's crazy. Meanwhile, the Pharisees reject him, thinking that his extraordinary power comes from the dark side. Today people demean him, saying he is "just" a great moral teacher or example of love. But someone who is "just" a moral teacher doesn't go around telling people that he can forgive sins. Jesus has an alternative explanation: *"The kingdom of God has come upon you."* In other words, the king is here.[2]

LOVE WALKED AMONG US

we act to get affirmation from people.
is that loving? NO because God ALREADY

✦ Saying "No" to Someone You Love *affirmed*

you!!

How might saying "no" work in our lives?

Jeff looks forward to going out to dinner Friday evening with his wife, Lois, and watching a movie afterward. Late Friday afternoon, Lois called Jeff and said, "Can I stay late at work tonight?" Jeff thought, "If I say 'no,' she'll use it against me." So he reluctantly said, "Okay, but try to get home early." After hearing Jeff's hesitation, Lois thought, "If I stay, he'll use it against me and whine all weekend." So after she got off the phone, she decided to come home. That evening Jeff was testy and a little grumpy. Things got tense between them.

When Lois called, Jeff didn't want to say "no" because it might look selfish. When she came home even after he told her she could stay late, he was irritated because he felt that Lois was making him appear selfish. Like George Wilson shouting at Dennis the Menace's father, he wanted to tell her, "I'm not the bad guy here. I'm the victim."

Now imagine Jesus inside Jeff. Lois calls and says, "Do you mind if I stay late tonight? I've got some things at work I want to finish up." The new Jeff can say "no" with great freedom. He is not afraid of Lois's rejection or of appearing selfish: "Lois, I'd really miss being with you tonight. I'd prefer you coming home." Nothing selfish here. Jeff honestly tells her his own good desires. Friday night has been a long-standing commitment with them. He loves being with her. Because Jeff has *the love of God in his heart*, he isn't going to be greatly bothered if Lois gives him the 'silent treatment' over dinner.

Or he could say, "Lois, I'd miss you, but if you want to stay, that is okay with me." Then he can tell himself that this is from God and wonder what might be in store for him. Later that evening, when he is alone and has a twinge of disappointment, he can trust that God has something better for him and look for it.

JESUS CARES FOR HIS MOTHER

As Jesus is slowly dying on the cross, his friends are watching from a distance:

> *Near the cross of Jesus stood his mother, his mother's sister, Mary the wife of Clopas, and Mary Magdalene. When Jesus saw his mother there, and the disciple whom he loved standing nearby, he said to his mother, "Dear woman, here is your son," and to the disciple, "Here is your mother." From that time on, this disciple took her into his home. (John 19:25-27)*

No mother wants to see her son die—let alone hang naked while slowly being tortured to death. We'd expect Mary to scream out "NO!" but she's silent. Gone is her agenda and suggestions. They have died. Almost certainly she reflects on what an old man in the temple said when she and Joseph brought Jesus there to be circumcised: *Simeon blessed them and said to Mary, his mother: ". . . a sword will pierce your own soul too" (Luke 2:34-35).*

Everything has gone wrong. Mary did not have this in mind when she pushed for Jesus' glory to be revealed at the wedding at Cana. But a week before his death Jesus had said, *"The hour has come for the Son of Man to be glorified" (John 12:23).* Who would have thought that Jesus' death (as we shall see later) was his time of glory, the time when God was most revealed through Jesus?

As she watches her son die, Mary's ego dies. The human ego, so strong and persistent, destroys love. We say "no" to those we love because of its presence. Silently standing with Jesus in his death, Mary surrenders control.

In all her previous encounters with Jesus, Mary moved to take control, but on the cross her son moves toward her. Even in his pain, his eyes search for his mother, and when he sees her, he cares for her future by asking his closest disciple, John, to bring her home.

134

Minutes later Jesus says, *"It is finished"* (*John 19:30*). Jesus' hour had finally come. Nothing more needs to be done. He has no regrets over missed opportunities, just a simple confidence that he has accomplished his mission. He can rest, even on the cross. His dependence on his Father not only anchors his relationships, but his soul as well.

CHAPTER THIRTEEN

SAYING "NO" TO SELF-GRATIFICATION

LOVE THAT IS PURE

*T*HE KIDS AND I WERE SITTING AROUND THE DINNER table while Jill was cleaning the kitchen. She likes to rinse the pots and pans before she sits down to eat so the food doesn't harden on them. I told her, "Come sit down. You can do that later. The kids are hungry." A minute passed and I said it again. And then again. She smelled a skunk in the basement and finally snapped back.

Jill had accurately sensed that I wasn't really concerned about the kids; I was hungry and had used them as an excuse to gratify my hunger. My underlying message to Jill was: "If you would just be like me, your life would be so much easier." (Is that irritating or what?) Such selfishness destroys love. If we mix love and self, we don't get a mixture of love and self—we just get plain selfishness.

How can we say "no" to selfishness? Again, Jesus is our model. The gospel of Matthew tells about an encounter Jesus had with Satan in the wilderness, where three times Satan tries to convince Jesus to give in to selfish desires.

The idea of Satan might seem odd to some people—isn't Satan

a myth of primitive people who weren't as smart as we are? Our world—especially the American world—doesn't have a category for evil, so we get blindsided by evil's senseless and bizarre nature. We've been taught to believe that people are basically nice, and that problems come from a lack of education and from poverty. But if this is true, how could Germany, one of the most educated and "enlightened" nations in the world, support Hitler? We squirm because we don't have a category to make sense of it.

Jesus knew about evil.[1] Scripture describes not only evil's existence, but also its "personal" character. Satan, who embodies evil, doesn't come with horns and a tail; he is a personal being who sought equality with God.

Saying "No" to Self-Gratification

In the following clash, Satan and Jesus treat one another coldly. No pleasantries soften their dueling. Jesus' wary replies, like sword thrusts, are quick and to the point.

> *Then Jesus was led by the Spirit into the desert to be tempted by the devil. After fasting forty days and forty nights, he was hungry. The tempter came to him and said, "[Since] you are the Son of God, tell these stones to become bread."*
>
> *Jesus answered, "It is written: 'Man does not live on bread alone, but on every word that comes from the mouth of God.'"*
> *(Matthew 4:1-4)[2]*

Jesus has been in the desert for forty days and has not eaten anything. He's hungry! Under the guise of caring for Jesus, Satan suggests: "You're hungry. You have special powers. Use those powers to take care of hunger." Notice the little twist: "Since *you are the Son of God*," use your power to take care of yourself. Remain strong, like God.[3]

LOVE WALKED AMONG US

But Jesus isn't his own boss, so he quotes Scripture in response: *"Man does not live on bread alone but on every word that comes from the mouth of the LORD" (Deuteronomy 8:3)*. He points to God's words as a source of life. "Read your Bible, Satan. Life does not consist of only taking care of physical needs, but also of listening to my Father." His Father's will pointed him away from self-gratification and to accepting his limits as a human.

Saying "No" to Self-Promotion

So Satan tries a different tactic:

> *Then the devil took him to the holy city and had him stand on the highest point of the temple. "If you are the Son of God," he said, "throw yourself down. For it is written: 'He will command his angels concerning you, and they will lift you up in their hands, so that you will not strike your foot against a stone.'"*
>
> *Jesus answered him, "It is also written: 'Do not put the Lord your God to the test.'" (Matthew 4:5-7)*

Satan skillfully twists Jesus' earlier response, saying, "If God's will is so important to you, then trust him by jumping from the highest point of the temple. And you want to quote the Bible? Well, the Bible says that God will protect you. Read Psalm 91, Jesus." Satan encourages Jesus to put himself in a situation that requires God to protect him.

To do as Satan suggests would be a spectacular display of power that would instantly and publicly show everyone that Jesus is the Son of God. An equivalent demonstration of power today would be jumping from the Goodyear Blimp onto the Super Bowl field in front of a TV audience of forty million. But Jesus says "no" to fame, to instant popularity.

Jesus' childlike simplicity and razor-sharp answers dismember

139

Satan's subtleties. He points out that Satan has isolated this Scripture from others (*"It is also written"*), making it say what he wanted instead of listening to what God said. Jesus goes on to say that it is wrong to *put God to the test*, to demand that God fix a situation in a certain way and put yourself above God under the guise of looking spiritual. He tells Satan, "No, even as I trust God, I will not act on my own. My Father must show me when and where to trust him—even in spiritual matters." Even in matters of faith, Jesus waits for God.

Saying "No" to Power

Since the subtle approach hasn't worked, Satan takes off his mask the third time he speaks with Jesus.

> *Again, the devil took him to a very high mountain and showed him all the kingdoms of the world and their splendor. "All this I will give you," he said, "if you will bow down and worship me."*
>
> *Jesus said to him, "Away from me, Satan! For it is written: 'Worship the Lord your God, and serve him only.'"*
> *(Matthew 4:8-10)*

What happens when I get just a little glimpse of what Satan showed Jesus? I see a beautiful woman and I am drawn to her. I get a compliment—a little piece of glory—and I think how insightful the person was. Another person tells me something I don't like, and I wonder what's wrong with that person.

But what sucks me in repulses Jesus. He gets angry at the thought of worshiping any aspect of life other than his heavenly Father. He refuses the quick path to glory and power and sends Satan away.

Luke ends his account of the temptation of Jesus saying, *When the devil had finished all this tempting, he left him until an opportune time* (Luke 4:13). Like the bad guy in horror movies, Satan returns. But not as a person—we can infer his presence as he influences people.

LOVE WALKED AMONG US

Jesus Says "No" to the Desire for a Quick Fix

Later Jesus did appear in the temple, but instead of a spectacular show to make himself look good (as Satan suggested), he chased out the money changers. Angered,

> . . . the Jews demanded of him, "What miraculous sign can you show us to prove your authority to do all this?"
>
> Jesus answered them, "Destroy this temple, and I will raise it again in three days."
>
> The Jews replied, "It has taken forty-six years to build this temple, and you are going to raise it in three days?" But the temple he had spoken of was his body. (John 2:18-21)

In rabbinical literature, a sign was a supernatural event that established your authority as a rabbi—it didn't serve anyone; it just trumpeted your credentials.[4] The authorities say to Jesus, "Do a miracle for yourself. Live for our opinion of you." Like Satan's idea of turning the stone into bread, this is an invitation to separate power from love.

But instead of seeking prominence, Jesus points to his death. The sign that will demonstrate who he is will be his death and resurrection. As we shall see, saying "no" to Satan meant saying "yes" to suffering. The Jews did not think of the Messiah as a suffering king; they saw him as a conquering king. So, not long before his death, Jesus patiently explains to his disciples that he is not the kind of Messiah they have been hunting for:

> He then began to teach them that the Son of Man must suffer many things and be rejected by the elders, chief priests and teachers of the law, and that he must be killed and after three days rise again. He spoke plainly about this, and Peter took him aside and began to rebuke him.

141

But when Jesus turned and looked at his disciples, he rebuked Peter. "Get behind me, Satan!" he said. "You do not have in mind the things of God, but the things of men."

Then he called the crowd to him along with his disciples and said, "If anyone would come after me, he must deny himself and take up his cross and follow me. For whoever wants to save his life will lose it, but whoever loses his life for me and for the gospel will save it." (Mark 8:31-35)

Upset by Jesus' words, Peter thinks: Messiahs don't die; they ride at the head of conquering armies and destroy the enemies of Israel. They use their power to get rid of people who make life difficult. If we could just get rid of Romans, life would be so much simpler. Why this talk about death, Jesus? Don't put yourself down. Know your worth. Where's your self-esteem? You're the Messiah, Jesus!

But Jesus turns and looks at the other disciples, so they can hear his rebuke to Peter. Like the religious leaders, Peter wants a Messiah who will make his world comfortable and pain-free. Satan is back, quietly suggesting thoughts, using Peter's small view of success to try to keep Jesus from the cross. But Jesus says "no." He will have nothing to do with quick, self-directed, and self-willed earthly success. This world is not his home: his life is with his heavenly Father. *"For I have come down from heaven not to do my will but to do the will of him who sent me" (John 6:38).*

Jesus' determination to obey his Father meant he would suffer. Such is the way of love.

Saying "No" to Self Invites Suffering

Instinctively, we fear a commitment to love because it means the end of so much. We wonder, "If I love like this, who will be there to love me?" Satan was playing into this worry when he tempted Jesus.

He wanted him to think, "If I don't take care of myself, no one else will," but Jesus doesn't cave in, because he trusts his Father's care.

When Robertson McQuilkin resigned his university presidency to care for his wife, friends urged him, "Muriel doesn't know you anymore, doesn't know anything, really, so it's time to put her in a nursing home and get on with life." When a student asked Robertson if he ever tired of caring for Muriel, he replied:

> "Tired? Every night. That's why I go to bed."
>
> "No, I mean tired of . . . " and she tilted her head toward Muriel, who sat silently in her wheelchair, her vacant eyes saying, "No one at home just now."
>
> "Why, no, I don't get tired. I love to care for her. She's my precious."[5]

Robertson chose love over self-fulfillment. However, many people end a relationship if it isn't meeting their needs. Their love evaporates if the relationship is not mutual, if it's not physical, if the other person doesn't communicate, or if one party isn't carrying his or her share of the load.[6]

But if our love depends on how the other person loves us, then we have a business deal, not love. Jesus said, "*If you love those who love you, what reward will you get? Are not even the tax collectors doing that?*" (*Matthew 5:46*). Is a pure, selfless love like this possible? Or are we always in it for ourselves?

Robertson tells about attending a workshop where . . .

> an expert told us that there were two reasons people keep a family member at home rather than in a nursing facility: economic necessity or feelings of guilt. Afterwards I spoke with her privately, trying to elicit some other possible motive for keeping someone at home. But she insisted those were the

143

only two motives. Finally I asked, "What about love?" "Oh," she replied, "We put that under guilt."[7]

Ironically, while our world is reluctant to call something evil, it has also grown cynical about the possibility of unselfish love. The denial of Satan's existence comes out of a mind-set that denies the reality of the spiritual world. But if the world is purely material, then all action is interpreted as self-centered and we have no basis for love. The denial of evil eventually leads to the assumption that there is no love.

JESUS SAYS "NO" TO HIMSELF
IN ORDER TO LOVE

Robertson McQuilkin relieved his wife's suffering by, in a sense, taking it on himself. Jesus told his disciples that he would *give his life as a ransom for many (Mark 10:45)*. To remove evil from the world he would suffer, taking evil on himself.

The night before his death, Jesus prays in a grove of olive trees called Gethsemane (which means "olive press"—olives were crushed under a stone pillar to extract the oil). Words can't do justice to the intense agony Jesus experiences in the olive grove as he anticipates the pain and suffering he's about to undergo. He's "distressed"—that pressured, restless, half-distracted state produced by mental stress. Crushed by grief, with no relief in sight. The intense pain shocks Jesus.[8] He speaks to his three friends, *"My soul is overwhelmed with sorrow to the point of death" (Mark 14:34)*. The pain is so intense that it is like death itself. Going a little farther into the grove, Jesus falls to the ground and prays, *"Abba, Father,"* he says, *"everything is possible for you. Take this cup from me. Yet not what I will, but what you will"* (Mark 14:35-36). Jesus wants relief from the coming terror. He asks for a way out. Nevertheless, he will be ruled by his Father and not his feelings: *"Yet not what I will, but what you will."*

144

Jesus Says "No" in His Darkest Hour

A few hours later, as Jesus is dying on the cross, he is tempted once more to do his own will. The crucifixion takes place on the Joppa road, the main road to the west, so there are many passersby.

> *Those who passed by hurled insults at him, shaking their heads and saying, "You who are going to destroy the temple and build it in three days, save yourself! Come down from the cross, if you are the Son of God!"*
>
> *In the same way, the chief priests, the teachers of the law and the elders mocked him. "He saved others," they said, "but he can't save himself! He's the king of Israel! Let him come down now from the cross, and we will believe in him. He trusts in God. Let God rescue him now if he wants him, for he said, 'I am the Son of God.'"* (Matthew 27:39-43)

"*If you are the Son of God, come down!*" cry some who passed by. "If you are God, then take care of yourself! Check out, Jesus. Use your power to protect yourself from pain. Use your divinity to protect your humanity."

"*You saved others, but you can't save yourself!*" they taunt. Jesus healed the sick and defended the weak, but who is going to defend him?

They continue to jeer. "*He trusts in God. Let God rescue him.* Look where you end up when you trust God like a little child. He abandons you, Jesus. You surrender yourself to God, and he takes advantage of you, sticking you up on this cross."

As Jesus presses up against the nails to catch his breath, his raw back scraping against the wood, the teachers and elders scream at him to do a sign. They tell him that if he will jump from the cross, then they will believe him.

But Jesus will have none of it. He will not turn inward and

145

seek human glory, nor be ruled by his feelings. He says "no" to his own desires. He trusts. He loves to the end.

CHAPTER FOURTEEN

SAYING "YES" TO GENTLE INTRUSION

LOVE BRINGS LIGHT INTO DARKNESS

ONE MORNING OUR DAUGHTER ASHLEY WAS particularly grumpy. Partly it was our strict curfew, partly it was a bad-hair day, and partly it was living with seven people who weren't constantly in touch with her needs. She was becoming increasingly self-absorbed, and as a result, constantly irritated with life.

After Ashley left for school, Jill began to think about how bad Ashley's attitude had been the last few months. She thought about going to the school, pulling Ashley out of class and talking to her. Finally, she told herself, "This is nuts," got in the car, drove to school, and told the principal, "I have something very important to talk about with my daughter."

Ashley was in the middle of tenth-grade choir practice, and the next thing she knew she was sitting in the parking lot in our minivan with her mother. Jill flipped down the mirror on the visor in front of Ashley and, with tears streaming down her face, said quietly, "Look at yourself. Do you know what you've become? Just look at yourself. Look at the jewelry. Look at the makeup. Look at your hairspray. Look at your boyfriend's bracelet. Now, look at your heart and compare your outside and your inside. One is fancy and the other is ugly."

Ashley told me later that she was so shocked that since then she has seldom worn jewelry or makeup. She would be the first to say that there is nothing wrong with makeup or jewelry. It's just that from then on she began to think about who she was on the inside. I now marvel at what Ashley finds beautiful. Not only does she surround herself with disabled people in her work as a Special Ed teacher, but the disabled are her friends outside of work.

Love moves toward people, even if that means confrontation. It doesn't leave them alone in their suffering or in their selfishness. Sometimes people are so paralyzed that unless we intrude, unless we break through both of our natural reserves, we can't love them. When I need to talk to one of our teenagers about something and know I'll get an earful, I remind myself that love moves toward people. I don't even need to know what to say—I can just move closer.

LOVE DOESN'T LEAVE PEOPLE ALONE

The same freedom Jesus has in saying "no" expresses itself in his gentle intrusions. Because he is anchored in his Father, he is neither captured by his culture's agenda nor afraid to have his own. Watch Jesus move in love toward this first-century "bad guy":

> Jesus entered Jericho and was passing through. A man was there by the name of Zacchaeus; he was a chief tax collector and was wealthy. He wanted to see who Jesus was, but being a short man he could not, because of the crowd. So he ran ahead and climbed a sycamore-fig tree to see him, since Jesus was coming that way.

When Jesus reached the spot, he looked up and said to him, "Zacchaeus, come down immediately. I must stay at your house today." So he came down at once and welcomed him gladly. All the people saw this and began to mutter, "He has gone to be the guest of a 'sinner.'"

But Zacchaeus stood up and said to the Lord, "Look, Lord! Here and now I give half of my possessions to the poor, and if I have cheated anybody out of anything, I will pay back four times the amount."

Jesus said to him, "Today salvation has come to this house, because this man, too, is a son of Abraham. For the Son of Man came to seek and to save what was lost." (Luke 19:1-10)

When I think of Zacchaeus, I see Danny DeVito—someone short, crooked, and a little flamboyant. As an employee of the Roman government who made himself rich by skimming the tax money, Zacchaeus was ostracized from Jewish society. He's scum. And since he manages the local tax collectors, he's a crook managing other crooks. His mere presence disgusts his fellow Jews because he is a reminder that they are an occupied country. Roman soldiers stand next to his tollbooth, enforcing his collections.

But Jesus boldly intrudes into Zacchaeus's life. He stops and looks up at him, and then invites himself over for dinner and to stay the night. This is similar to the President stopping his motorcade to say he's coming to your house—Jesus is the hottest thing to hit Israel in a few hundred years. If you were Zacchaeus, you'd be honored. Yet I doubt that the President would say "I *must* stay" or "come down *immediately*" (literally, "hurry up"). Jesus speaks with authority, expecting to be obeyed as if he were a king. The power of his miracles matches the power of his person.

But in the first century "good people" didn't eat with tax collectors because a meal was not just about eating; it was a sharing of life.

Jesus' willingness to eat with Zacchaeus told everyone that Jesus not only accepted the tax collector, he also forgave him. This disgusts the crowd. Jesus has broken a social taboo.

When we love, we get dirty. Jesus loved the widow of Nain and became "unclean" by touching the casket. Here the dirt comes from the opinions of people who look down on Jesus for associating with someone who has stolen from his fellow Jews and divided their money between himself and the Roman government.

Getting wind of people's gossip, Zacchaeus fixes the bad reputation he's given Jesus by improving his own reputation. He spontaneously commits himself to more than full restitution and to giving away half his wealth. A perfect manager, Zacchaeus goes to the heart of the problem and fixes it so thoroughly that it can't come back. First Jesus takes on Zacchaeus' burden; then Zacchaeus takes on Jesus' burden. By inviting himself to dinner, Jesus created a chain of love that now reaches hundreds of poor people.

Why does Jesus intrude? He's on a God-directed mission to seek and save what was lost. Jesus sought out Zacchaeus. He didn't just wait for people to come to him. He is an invading king, coming to get his kingdom. Jesus began his life's work announcing that God was now gently intruding into the world. *"The kingdom of God is near"* (Mark 1:14). So like a king, Jesus moves in and takes charge. But what a strange kingdom: the poor, outcasts, prostitutes, Samaritans, and women! No wonder Jesus told Pilate, *"My kingdom is not of this world"* (John 18:36). It's an upside-down kingdom.

With a final touch of love, Jesus turns and blesses Zacchaeus: *"Today salvation has come to this house"* (Luke 19:9). Jesus' name in Hebrew means "God saves." Jesus saved Zacchaeus by associating with him, thus taking upon himself Zacchaeus' bad reputation. Salvation worked by substitution: that's how love works.

LOVE WALKED AMONG US

Touch As an Intrusion of Love

Princess Diana amazed people because of her willingness to touch a dirty, impoverished child or hold an AIDS-infected baby in her arms. She was regal, elegant, yet she had a human touch. The mourning at her death was unprecedented. By touching people physically, she touched us emotionally. The same was true with Mother Teresa. The image of her holding a destitute and dying person—not repelled by the squalor of feces, vomit, sputum, and blood—elicited love and admiration from the whole world. Mother Teresa said, "We train ourselves to be extremely kind and gentle in touch of hand, tone of voice, and in our smile, so as to make the mercy of God very real." She consciously imitated Jesus' touch.[1]

When Jesus touched people, he gently intruded into their lives. Whatever he touched became clean and whole. He touched the blind, the deaf, and the lame when he healed them. He moved toward people that others pulled away from. He couldn't seem to keep his hands off lepers:

> While Jesus was in one of the towns, a man came along who was covered with leprosy. When he saw Jesus, he fell with his face to the ground and begged him, "Lord, if you are willing, you can make me clean."
>
> Filled with compassion, Jesus reached out his hand and touched the man. "I am willing," he said. "Be clean!" Immediately the leprosy left him and he was cured. (Luke 5:12; Mark 1:41)

Leprosy disfigures its victims by destroying their ability to feel pain. Lepers "lose" limbs because they don't know when they've hurt themselves. Their appearance frightened people. People also feared "catching" this contagious disease. If a person got leprosy, he was ostracized from his family, never to have physical contact with them again, never to hug his children or feel the caresses of a spouse. When anyone came near him, he had to call out, "Unclean, unclean." Jews were forbidden to touch a leper. Lepers were "unclean" in every sense of the word.

Knowing all this, Jesus puts his hand on the leper's mangled, infected face. In an instant it becomes clean and whole, like the skin of a baby. In an instant Jesus gives back to this man his body, his family, and his people.

Sometimes Jesus touched people when they were just afraid or confused. Once when the disciples were paralyzed with fear Jesus came and touched them. *"Get up," he said. "Don't be afraid" (Matthew 17:7).* After he healed a little boy, *"Jesus took him by the hand and lifted him to his feet" (Mark 9:27).*

An ancient prophecy about the Messiah reflected this tenderness: *He will not shout or cry out, or raise his voice in the streets. A bruised reed he will not break, and a smoldering wick he will not snuff out (Isaiah 42:2-3).* The Messiah would not be loud or aggressive. He would gently handle people who were like bruised reeds, which only the slightest touch would snap, and would tenderly care for people who were like candles that were barely lit, which the least movement would extinguish.

Often we're afraid to touch because, whether it's physical or figurative, touching risks violating personal space and presumes intimacy. We never know what we'll get into or how we'll be misinterpreted. There are plenty of modern "lepers": the disabled, the lonely, the mentally ill. A friend of mine whose wife struggles with depression said, "Everyone asks me how my wife is doing, but no one visits her." But love brings light into the darkness. It intrudes.

Of course, some people touch inappropriately. When talking about the danger of sexual lust, Jesus exaggerates for the sake of emphasis, *"If your right hand causes you to sin, cut if off" (Matthew 5:30).* Our hands are meant to gently touch with love. How can you even think of using your hands to touch people as objects?

SELFLESS OPENNESS

It's tough to love people when they constantly come into your space, demanding attention. But if we are always in control, deciding whom and when we will love, then we risk having a weak imitation of love. If we aren't open to our schedule being interrupted or our bank account tapped, then we might be fooling ourselves as to our own goodness. Love gives.

Jesus selflessly opens his life to the needs of the least, the lost, the lonely, and the lepers. He not only touches them, he also lets them touch him. For instance: the woman in Simon's house wept at Jesus' feet, drying his feet with her hair. At the Last Supper John asks Jesus a whispered question as he leans back against him. This moment was so moving for John that he calls himself the one who leaned back against Jesus at the supper (John 13:25).

Watch this intrusion inside an intrusion:

Now when Jesus returned, a crowd welcomed him, for they were all expecting him. Then a man named Jairus, a ruler of the synagogue, came and fell at Jesus' feet, pleading with him to come to his house because his only daughter, a girl of about twelve, was dying.

As Jesus was on his way, the crowds almost crushed him. And a woman was there who had been subject to bleeding for twelve years, but no one could heal her. She came up behind him and touched the edge of his cloak, and immediately her bleeding stopped.

He turned around in the crowd and asked, "Who touched my clothes?"

When they all denied it, Peter said, "Master, the people are crowding and pressing against you."

But Jesus said, "Someone touched me; I know that power has gone out from me." He kept looking around to see who had done it.

Then the woman, seeing that she could not go unnoticed, came trembling and fell at his feet. In the presence of all the people, she told

153

*why she had touched him and how she had been instantly healed.
Then he said to her, "Daughter, your faith has healed you. Go in
peace."*

*While Jesus was still speaking, someone came from the house
of Jairus, the synagogue ruler. "Your daughter is dead," he said.
"Don't bother the teacher any more."*

*Hearing this, Jesus said to Jairus, "Don't be afraid; just believe,
and she will be healed."*

*When he arrived at the house of Jairus, he did not let anyone go
in with him except Peter, John and James, and the child's father and
mother. Meanwhile, all the people were wailing and mourning for her.
"Stop wailing," Jesus said. "She is not dead but asleep."*

They laughed at him, knowing that she was dead.

*But he took her by the hand and said, "My child, get up!" Her
spirit returned, and at once she stood up. Then Jesus told them to give
her something to eat. (Luke 8:40-55; Mark 5:30,32)*

As Jesus comes home from an exhausting trip to a warm welcome and a well-deserved rest, the leader of the local synagogue
interrupts him because his daughter is dying. As Jesus goes to help,
the large crowds almost crush him. An "unclean" woman, forbidden
to enter Jairus's synagogue because of her menstrual flow, works
her way through the large crowd to Jesus. Anyone she touched
would be ceremonially unclean for a day (Leviticus 15:26-27).
Because of her impurity and inability to have children she is almost
certainly either divorced or unmarried—she's a female leper. If
she openly asks Jesus to heal her, she will invite more shame from
people who are disgusted by her condition. So when she reaches
Jesus, she just touches one of the blue tassels that Jewish men wore
at the corner of their garments. Instantly, she is healed.

Jesus stops and looks around. "Who touched me?" Peter points
out the absurdity of Jesus' question, because *the people are crowding
and pressing against* him—making the crowd's denial a little comical

as well. (This gives us a glimpse of what it felt like to be Jesus—constantly being interrupted and touched.) But Jesus says this wasn't a normal touch.

Usually, Jesus looks first and then heals. But the woman's actions force Jesus to reverse his normal pattern. He looks for her after he heals her. Jesus never heals without connecting with a person, never separates his power from his love. So he delays an emergency. Knowing she is about to be caught, the woman emerges from the crowd and publicly describes her life of pain and shame as Jesus silently listens. He commends her willingness to come to him empty and her confidence that his power would be for her. Finally, he blesses her: "Go in peace. Shalom to you for the rest of your life."

Then Jesus' second interruption (the woman) gets interrupted by his first interruption (Jairus). Word has come to Jairus that it's too late—his daughter is dead. Unlike the woman's, Jairus's faith falters. Dead people don't come back to life. But Jesus reassures him, and they go to the daughter.

When the mourners hear that Jesus thinks she's only sleeping, they interrupt their mourning for a good laugh. You can tell they are professional mourners—only a pro could go from weeping to laughing and back again. Ever in charge, Jesus orders the mourners out of the house: "I will not have you in this house messing up this very special moment for the parents. You don't believe. You don't see." Then he takes the girl by the hand and raises her from the dead. The stunned parents don't know what to do. Jesus, always practical, always thinking of the person, tells them she's famished and to get her something to eat.

THE BALANCE OF LOVE

Jesus says "no" to some intrusions but welcomes others, and then turns around and intrudes into others' lives. But love is like that—

it's not rigid. How can we know when to intrude and when not? The following story suggests some ways.

Jill was frustrated. Our part-time tax business was down by twenty customers. She came home from grocery shopping and was discouraged by how tight our budget was. She told me that she didn't even have money to buy hand cream. I immediately offered to buy her some hand cream with money I'd saved on the side. Jill ignored my offer, saying that we'd been tight for ten years, and she was sick of it. She told me to go on vacation by myself—that would save a few bucks. We were both mad.

Later that evening I was depressed because of our argument. I was angry with Jill and overwhelmed with our finances. I realized I couldn't do anything about our finances. I needed God to move in and take charge of how I related to Jill. I found myself praying, asking for help because I didn't know what to do. Then it dawned on me that Jill just wanted me to listen. Being financially tight is a pain, and it's not likely that anything I could say would fix that.

The next morning I told her that I was sorry for trying to "fix" her and for giving her quick answers. She responded, "Why do you love me so poorly?"

I repeated my apology and added, "I know it wasn't just the hand cream." But I also said that I really had been working on trying to love her. Then I waited a bit and told her, "When you are afraid, you become aggressive. Just tell me how lousy it feels to always be tight financially. Tell me what you are afraid of instead of coming on strong."

Jill was quiet.

The "key" that unlocked a typically muddled argument was my prayer for guidance. Talking to God shone a light on my dirt and allowed me to take my eyes off "what she said." I looked like I was helping Jill, but I was really helping myself—I wanted her to stop pressuring me. Her distress made me uncomfortable, and I wanted that feeling to go away. Giving her a quick solution was an easy way to try to get her to be quiet.

Neither of us was willing to feel a certain way. Jill thought, "I will not feel helpless because we don't have enough money, so I'll hassle you." I thought, "I will not feel unsettled by our lack of money. I will not let you hassle me so I will give quick solutions." Instead of accepting Jill's intrusion, I rejected it. I should have told her "yes" instead of "no."

In the morning when I apologized to Jill for not listening to her, I was opening myself up to her intrusion. When we apologize, people don't always say, "That's okay. It's just wonderful you apologized." Openness is risky. But I was sure of God's love for me, so it was safe to agree with Jill that at times I loved her poorly. It's true.

I also quietly said "no." Jill said I had loved her poorly. I told her that I had been growing in my love for her. Then when I asked her to share her fears with me I was gently intruding.

Even if we understand all the principles of love, we still might intrude when we should wait or wait when we should intrude. We need a third will (God's) to shape our will and teach us how to love.

PART 4
LOVE IS ENERGIZED BY FAITH

Chapter Fifteen

FAITH EMPOWERS LOVE

Where Can I Find the Energy to Love?

YOU'RE LATE GETTING OUT OF WORK, SO YOU call ahead and ask your husband to start the laundry, your son to do his homework, and your daughter to throw the casserole in the oven. When you walk in the door your husband is plopped on the sofa, watching TV, and the laundry basket is sitting where you left it; your son is glued to the computer as his book bag sits in the corner, unopened; and your daughter is on the phone as the frozen casserole sits on the counter. No one looks up as you come in. You want to scream. Love is the farthest thing from your mind. You think, "When is someone going to love me and anticipate my needs?"

The hardest part of love is not, "How do I love?"; it's wanting to love in the first place, and then having the energy to do it. It takes energy to love, energy that we don't often have.

Jesus said he was energized by his Father: *"I live because of the Father"* (*John* 6:57). The word for that simple dependence on God is "faith." Scratch whatever preexisting definitions of faith you may have, such as trusting something that is opposed to reason or doesn't make sense. For Jesus, faith is a life-connection with his Father that affects every relationship. We all have "faith" in something, because we all depend on someone or something—even if it's ourselves.

Let's look at a day in the life of Jesus, one year before his death, where we see him grapple with the problem of the energy needed for love. That all four gospels record this remarkable day shows that it shook the disciples to their roots.

THE MORNING: AN INTERRUPTED REST

It is springtime in Galilee, a Friday morning about the time of Passover—a beautiful time in Palestine. But clouds are on the horizon. News just arrived that King Herod has killed John the Baptist, Jesus' cousin. John had denounced Herod for marrying his brother's wife. Many had thought John might be the Messiah. Revolution is in the air.

Hundreds of years before, Jewish prophets predicted the coming of the Messiah (the Greek word is *Christ*), a person from God who would save Israel and, in some strange way, all of humanity as well. Jewish people had been waiting for the Messiah for hundreds of years. Even some educated Romans expected that a world deliverer was going to come out of Palestine.[1]

Jesus' popularity has skyrocketed. *So many people were coming and going that they did not even have a chance to eat.* So Jesus suggests to his disciples a short break on the other side of the lake. *"Come with me by yourselves to a quiet place and get some rest." So they went away by themselves in a boat to a solitary place (Mark 6:31-32).* The other side of the lake is out of Herod's territory, taking Jesus out of danger.[2]

In addition to physical rest, Jesus invites his disciples to a deeper, soul rest: *"Come to me, all you who are weary and burdened, and I will give you rest" (Matthew 11:28).* But their retreat is short-lived.

LOVE WALKED AMONG US

*Many who saw them leaving recognized them and ran on foot from
all the towns and got there ahead of them. When Jesus landed and
saw a large crowd, he had compassion on them, because they were
like sheep without a shepherd. So he began teaching them many
things. (Mark 6:33-34)*

Jesus looks at the crowd, feels compassion, and then begins
teaching. He begins the day retreating (saying "no"), and then
he moves toward the crowd, letting their desires—and deeper
needs—shape his agenda (saying "yes").

The Afternoon: Meager Resources

As the sun begins to set over the Sea of Galilee, Jesus says to Philip,

*"Where shall we buy bread for these people to eat?" He asked this
only to test him, for he already had in mind what he was going to
do.*
   *Philip answered him, "Eight months' wages would not buy
enough bread for each one to have a bite!"*
   *Another of his disciples, Andrew, Simon Peter's brother, spoke
up, "Here is a boy with five small barley loaves and two small fish,
but how far will they go among so many?" (John 6:5-9)*

Jesus faces the disciples with an overwhelming need: feeding
thousands of hungry people with only five loaves of bread and two
fish. He wants them to ask for help, to think outside the human
box, and to turn to him in the same way that he turns to his Father.
   Philip responds with typical frankness: "No way!" Andrew mentions their meager resources: Barley was the food of the poor, and
the dried fish were small, like our sardines.

163

> *Then Jesus directed them to have all the people sit down in groups on the green grass. So they sat down in groups of hundreds and fifties. Taking the five loaves and the two fish and looking up to heaven, he gave thanks and broke the loaves. Then he gave them to his disciples to set before the people. He also divided the two fish among them all. They all ate and were satisfied, and the disciples picked up twelve basketfuls of broken pieces of bread and fish. The number of the men who had eaten was five thousand. (Mark 6:39-44)*

Jesus feeds the people because they are hungry. Plain and simple. But the actions are also a parable, demonstrating that he is the source of life. *The people sit down. . . on the green grass.* Note how similar the wording is to Psalm 23: *"The LORD is my shepherd, I shall not be in want. He makes me lie down in green pastures."* Jesus then *prepares a table before them* and gives them so much that their *cup overflows* with twelve baskets of leftovers. Jesus creates an overflowing abundance out of a pittance, similar to what he did with the wine at the wedding in Cana. *Goodness and mercy* have pursued the people in the person of Jesus. They have been cared for by a loving shepherd.

What is it like to know that no matter how messed up you might be, the good shepherd looks at you with love, surrounds you with his compassion, envelops you in his arms, and cares for the details of your life? Love begins, not with loving, but with being loved. Being loved gives you the freedom and the resources to love. We can only give what we have received.

Faith at its simplest is receiving love, trusting that we will be safe with someone. Jesus' actions tell the crowd that he is worthy of their trust. If they will come to him, he will care for them. But they don't want to depend on him, they want to control him.

After Dinner: Seizing the Energy of God

After the crowd had eaten, *immediately Jesus made his disciples get into the boat and go on ahead of him to Bethsaida, while he dismissed the crowd (Mark 6:45)*. Why might he remove the disciples and dismiss such a huge crowd by himself? The disciples would be overwhelmed with the coming temptation to make Jesus king: *After the people saw the miraculous sign that Jesus did, they began to say, 'Surely this is the Prophet who is to come into the world.' Jesus, knowing that they intended to come and make him king by force, withdrew again to a mountain by himself to pray (John 6:14-15; Mark 6:46)*.

The crowd would have remembered Moses' prophesy that there would come a prophet like himself (Deuteronomy 18:15). First-century Jews anticipated that the Messiah would re-enact the story of Israel. Just as Moses provided the Israelites bread in their desert wanderings, so would the Messiah also provide bread. He would do what Moses did, only better.

The people think: "This is the sign we've been waiting for. Jesus is the king! He's the long anticipated descendant of King David, who will rule an earthly kingdom of Israel. Seize the moment. Drive the Romans into the sea."

They didn't long for a Messiah simply for political reasons, they had personal reasons as well. Likely some had crops that had done poorly that spring, and this was the first solid meal they'd had in months. Others may have been accosted by a Roman soldier just the week before. Still others had been healed by Jesus. They think: "It is all so clear. And if Jesus resists, well, we'll just force him."

The crowd saw Jesus as the answer to their problems, and they tried to remake him in their own image. They wanted a God who would make their lives pleasant—"If I just had a million dollars . . . If only my husband would listen . . . If only my wife would stop nagging . . . If only . . . "

Once again Satan is back, offering a carefree, easy solution to the problems of this world: Jesus, the walking welfare state, the ultimate

165

bread-making machine. It is an intoxicating view of the kingdoms of this world, but Jesus isn't buying it. He shoves the disciples into the boat. A true king, not swept along by the crowd, he rules by dismissing them.

If human nature is basically okay, then the crowd's demand for Jesus to be a human king makes sense, because only surface, cosmetic change is needed: political reform, better education, or more jobs. But if the influence of evil is pervasive, if it is within each person, then a more radical solution is necessary. If the problem is the human heart, and not the Romans, then the human heart needs a new king. Isn't that why we find love difficult? We want to be the ruler, to be in control, to have another serve us. Instead of "doing nothing on our own and doing just what our Father wants," we have ignored God, creating gods that make us feel good about ourselves. Faith is a return to God that says, "I've done it my way. I need help." Living independently of God cuts us off from the power to love and ultimately destroys love.

THE NEXT MORNING

Having dismissed the crowd, Jesus retreats to the mountain to talk with his Father. Later that night, he joins his disciples in the boat. The next morning when he arrives on the other side of the lake, at Capernaum, the same crowds greet his arrival. *When they found him on the other side of the lake, they asked him, "Rabbi, when did you get here?"* (John 6:25). But they really don't want to hear what Jesus has to say. They just want another free meal. Dinner was great; breakfast should be superb. Jesus exposes their motives: *"I tell you the truth, you are looking for me, not because you saw miraculous signs but because you ate the loaves and had your fill"* (John 6:26).

Jesus challenges the crowd to eat something that will really satisfy, instead of focusing on instant gratification: *"Do not work for food that spoils, but for food that endures to eternal life, which the Son of Man will give* you. On him God the Father has placed his seal of approval" (John 6:27). (Eternal life encompasses the idea of "really living" or "life-as-it-was-meant-to-be.") But the crowd wants a cosmic bellhop. They are trying to find life outside of God, in things. They think the answer is Jesus—not a messenger from God, but a Jesus of their own making. They just want Jesus to show them the five-step program. Then they asked him, "What must we do to do the works God requires?" Jesus answered, "The work of God is this: to believe in the one he has sent" (John 6:28-29).

Every would-be "Messiah"—there were at least a dozen in the first century—had asked his followers to believe on him. But if the people are going to trust Jesus to be their "man" to take on the Romans, they want a sign, a magical demonstration of Jesus' power. And what better sign than breakfast? So they asked him, "What miraculous sign then will you give that we may see it and believe you? What will you do? Our forefathers ate the manna in the desert; as it is written: 'He gave them bread from heaven to eat'" (John 6:30-31). Translation: "Moses gave our ancestors bread in the wilderness. Hint, hint, Jesus. Time for breakfast."

But Jesus has something better than breakfast. Jesus said to them, "I tell you the truth, it is not Moses who has given you the bread from heaven, but it is my Father who gives you the true bread from heaven. For the bread of God is he who comes down from heaven and gives life to the world" (John 6:32-33).

Jesus uses a human need to point to himself as a source of life. But the crowd misunderstands and is just gratified that Jesus is talking about bread again. And why stop at just breakfast? Let's go for the whole enchilada. Let's get a lifetime meal ticket. "Sir," they said, "from now on give us this bread" (verse 34).

Jesus unabashedly says that he is the solution to human need: Then Jesus declared, "I am the bread of life. He who comes to me will never go hungry, and he who believes in me will never be thirsty" (6:35). If some of Jesus' earlier actions were the equivalent of burning an American flag, this statement is like saying "I am the flag." Other first-century, would-be "Messiahs" didn't talk this way.

FAITH EMPOWERS LOVE

Later, when their conversation shifts to the synagogue in Capernaum, Jesus tells the crowd, *"Just as the living Father sent me and I live because of the Father, so the one who feeds on me will live because of me"* (6:57). He describes a chain of life where he is empowered by his Father, and his disciples, in turn, are empowered by him. He not only practices dependence, but also encourages his disciples to be dependent. Jesus isn't asking them to do anything that he isn't already doing.

Jesus asks the crowd to believe in him as a total life experience. Without that kind of faith, they will not be able to love. At another time, Jesus tells his disciples, *"Neither can you bear fruit [love] unless you remain in me [faith]"* (John 15:4).

A model of love, like Jesus, doesn't necessarily energize us to love. We might be inspired to love, but we don't necessarily change. A good model can leave us depressed, because it doesn't deal with our weariness with life. Many of us are just trying to get from one end of the day to the other. Neither does a model of love deal with our inward bent. Often we don't want a model for love—we just want to enjoy life and have other people see how reasonable we are. Or even better, we want "others" to learn how to love "us" and anticipate our every need.

Love is difficult. Jesus tells us to love not only our kids but also those who are beat-up, lying by the side of the road, and even our enemies! How is this possible? Go to God empty and tell him your needs, your inability to love. Jesus says, *"Come to me, all you who are weary and burdened, and I will give you rest"* (Matthew 11:28). Jesus shows us not only how to love, but also how to get the power to love. The one who commands love offers the power to love.

Once When I Stopped Demanding Breakfast

But what does faith look like? How can you and I *do* faith?

In a staff meeting, I was discussing a new project with two

coworkers. The meeting was winding down, and I realized that it wasn't clear to the other two that I was the one who had come up with the idea of the project. I immediately thought of a remedy: I would say something like, "When I first came up with the idea for this project . . . " I wouldn't directly boast, I'd just "clarify" something that would show it was my idea. (In other words, I was going to boast.)

But I didn't. I was quiet because it dawned on me that boasting was like asking Jesus to make breakfast. My food would have been trying to get them to like me. To want their approval was to *work for food that spoils*. It would leave me still hungry.

My two coworkers left the room, and the meeting ended without me saying anything. As I sat there alone, I felt an overwhelming sense of emptiness and pointlessness. Life didn't seem worth living. I was surprised at how strong the feeling was. I mean, all I did was not boast. Why the feeling?

I was feeling my heart, what life is like without God. Boasting gives us a false sense of "really living." Letting other people know how good we are is a not-so-subtle way of stealing love. When I stopped stealing (by not boasting), I felt my emptiness.

As I sat there, I became hungry for God. For real life. For food that sticks to the ribs. Nothing dramatic happened. But I walked out of that room full. I had a real meal instead of my junk-food boasting. I thought about Jesus' words to the crowd that Saturday morning: *"I tell you the truth, unless you eat the flesh of the Son of Man and drink his blood, you have no life in you"* (John 6:53).

If you find these words strange, you are not alone. Listen to the crowd's response:

> At this the Jews began to grumble about him because he said, "I am the bread that came down from heaven." They said, "Is this not Jesus, the son of Joseph, whose father and mother we know? How can he now say, 'I came down from heaven?'" (John 6:41-42)

FAITH EMPOWERS LOVE

We know this guy. We know his parents. Who does he think he is? God's gift to mankind?

It is too much for some.

> From this time many of his disciples turned back and no longer followed him.
>
> "You do not want to leave too, do you?" Jesus asked the Twelve.
>
> Simon Peter answered him, "Lord, to whom shall we go? You have the words of eternal life. We believe and know that you are the Holy One of God." (John 6:66-69)

CHAPTER SIXTEEN

FAITH MEANS
LOSING CONTROL

GOING TO GOD
WITH OUR NEEDS

N A RECENT FLIGHT I ASKED MY SEATMATE WHAT HE thought about a study of Jesus as a person. He said, "I'm the wrong person to ask. I'm an atheist." His honesty intrigued me. Many people behave as if God doesn't exist, but few actually say they are atheists. Curious, I asked him why. He went on to tell me about his son's disability. He could not believe in a God that would permit such suffering. I just listened; we had a lot in common.

I told him about Kim and about how her faith has given her courage and strength. She says that Jesus is with her during the day. She quickly turns to him—a living, present, and active Jesus—for help when things get rough. Just as we were landing, my seatmate wondered, half to himself, if he had hurt his son by not mentioning God.

The disciples didn't put their faith in Jesus all at once. They went through a series of stages, almost like falling in love. Every time they thought they had Jesus figured out, he'd break out of their mold. Coming to understand Jesus was also inseparable from coming to understand themselves. To see Jesus was to see their inadequacy. That happened the day they decided to follow him.

Rethinking the Relationship

Jesus had been speaking to a crowd by the shore of the Sea of Galilee, while Peter and his companions were washing their nets nearby. Jesus asked to borrow their boat, so he could speak more effectively to a larger number of people without being crushed. We have a good idea of the size of the boat because archaeologists have recently uncovered a sixteen-foot, first-century fishing boat buried in the mud by the Sea of Galilee.

When [Jesus] had finished speaking, he said to Simon, "Put out into deep water, and let down the nets for a catch." Simon answered, "Master, we've worked hard all night and haven't caught anything. But because you say so, I will let down the nets" (Luke 5:4-5). You can sense Peter's patient exasperation with Jesus. "You do the preaching, and I'll do the fishing." Fishing is best on the Sea of Galilee by the inlets early in the morning or at night with torches. Any fisherman knows that fish don't bite at midday in the deep. But Peter gives it a shot anyway:

> *When they had done so, they caught such a large number of fish that their nets began to break. So they signaled their partners in the other boat to come and help them, and they came and filled both boats so full that they began to sink.*
>
> *When Simon Peter saw this, he fell at Jesus' knees and said, "Go away from me, Lord; I am a sinful man!" For he and all his companions were astonished at the catch of fish they had taken, and so were James and John, the Sons of Zebedee, Simon's partners.*
>
> *Then Jesus said to Simon, "Don't be afraid; from now on you will catch men." So they pulled their boats up on shore, left everything and followed him. (Luke 5:6-11)*

LOVE WALKED AMONG US

Prior to this, the disciples knew Jesus just as a teacher or rabbi. Now this perception is shattered. They soon conclude, along with the crowds, that Jesus is a prophet, a messenger from God (Luke 7:16; Mark 8:28). Like the ancient Hebrew prophets, encountering Jesus brought them in touch with God's holiness, which is unsettling. Yet at the same time, they are drawn to him so they respond to his call. In Mark's version of this incident (1:17), the Greek indicates that when Jesus calls them to become *fishers of men*, they will go through a process. But, just like falling in love, they had no idea what they were getting into.

LOSING CONTROL

Some months later, the disciples' view of Jesus is disturbed again when they're out in their boat and a storm comes up. Winds coming off the desert, combined with the low elevation of the Sea of Galilee (212 meters below sea level), create sudden, violent storms. Having taught all day, Jesus is exhausted, asleep in the back of the boat on a cushion ordinarily used by the person at the steering oar. Initially, the disciples are so busy trimming the sail and bailing water that they don't notice that Jesus is still sleeping. They wake him yelling, *"Don't you care if we drown?"* (Mark 4:38) At the very least he could help bail. Jesus gets up and in a clear, strong voice commands the winds and the waves:

> *"Quiet! Be still!" Then the wind died down and it was completely calm. He said to his disciples, "Why are you so afraid? Do you still have no faith?" They were terrified and amazed and asked each other, "Who is this? Even the wind and the waves obey him!" (Mark 4:39-41, also Matthew 8:27)*

The disciples are stunned. The storm scared them; but the calm terrified them. "Storms we understand. Jesus we don't." He doesn't fit any of their categories. It was one thing to catch a few fish; it is another to control vast storms instantly with a word. The idea of Jesus as a prophet does not take into account the power to calm an entire weather system. Something completely different is going on here, so they ask themselves, "Who is this man?" He disrupts their categories.

Jesus also challenges their lack of faith in him. They wanted someone to help bail, a partner. They didn't expect someone who could master the whole situation. They would just as soon not have that much help with their lives. Jesus has a way of taking control of every life he is invited into.

Following Jesus means losing control. The evening after feeding the five thousand, Jesus rejoins his disciples in the boat.

> During the fourth watch of the night Jesus went out to them, walking on the lake. When the disciples saw him walking on the lake, they were terrified. "It's a ghost," they said, and cried out in fear.
>
> But Jesus immediately said to them: "Take courage! It is I. Don't be afraid."
>
> "Lord, if it's you," Peter replied, "tell me to come to you on the water."
>
> "Come," he said.
>
> Then Peter got down out of the boat, walked on the water and came toward Jesus. But when he saw the wind, he was afraid and, beginning to sink, cried out, "Lord, save me!"
>
> Immediately Jesus reached out his hand and caught him. "You of little faith," he said, "why did you doubt?"
>
> And when they climbed into the boat, the wind died down. Then those who were in the boat worshiped him, saying, "Truly you are the Son of God." (Matthew 14:25-32)

The disciples' view of Jesus continues to expand. They are beginning to conclude that Jesus is far more than a prophet.[1] At

LOVE WALKED AMONG US

the same time, Jesus' message is simple: "Peter, when you look away from me and at your circumstances, you will become afraid and begin to sink. You must keep your eyes on me. I am enough." He wants Peter to look at him when it's storming, just as he wanted Philip to look at him when there wasn't enough food for the crowd. This is how to find the energy for life, including love.

In love, Jesus looked at people. In faith, we look to Jesus.

GOING TO JESUS WITH YOUR NEED

Only a few weeks later, Jesus and the disciples again snatch some quiet moments together while sailing across the lake. Away from the demanding crowds, with only the gentle lapping of the oars to interrupt their conversation, Jesus warns them about the *yeast* of the Pharisees, who have just asked Jesus for another sign.

> *The disciples had forgotten to bring bread, except for one loaf they had with them in the boat. "Be careful," Jesus warned them. "Watch out for the yeast of the Pharisees and that of Herod."*
>
> *They discussed this with one another and said, "It is because we have no bread."*
>
> *Aware of their discussion, Jesus asked them: "Why are you talking about having no bread? Do you still not see or understand? Are your hearts hardened? Do you have eyes but fail to see, and ears but fail to hear? And don't you remember? When I broke the five loaves for the five thousand, how many basketfuls of pieces did you pick up?"*
>
> *"Twelve," they replied.*
>
> *"And when I broke the seven loaves for the four thousand, how many basketfuls of pieces did you pick up?"*
>
> *They answered, "Seven."*
>
> *He said to them, "Do you still not understand?"*
>
> *(Mark 8:14-21)*

Jesus' reference to the *yeast of the Pharisees and Herod* is symbolic. In Jewish culture yeast symbolized something unclean that pervaded the whole. The "unclean" Pharisees appeared to be trusting in God when they were actually trusting in themselves.

But the disciples miss the symbolism. They hear *yeast* and think *bread*. "Someone forgot to order the pizza! How can we have a party without pizza?" They panic, and thinking with their stomachs, assume that Jesus is upset they've forgotten lunch.

This irritates Jesus. He sounds just like a mom whose son has forgotten to bring his lunch to school for three days in a row, "How many times do I have to tell you to put your lunch in your book bag?"

But Jesus is not upset about the missing bread, nor is he upset that they misunderstood him. Jesus is upset that when faced with a need, the disciples looked to themselves instead of turning to him. "Were you sleeping when I made ten thousand loaves of bread? Don't you think I can do the same thing now?" They're behaving as if Jesus is powerless to help them. They had compartmentalized their lives: "Jesus only makes bread when there is a crisis or when there are huge crowds of people, Jesus will do something unique." They had put his two feeding miracles into a spiritual category.

The disciples are worried about not having bread, but they have a walking bread factory in the boat. They are dying for a drink while leaning with a pocket full of change against a soda machine. "Did you see the abundance, the number of baskets left over? Don't you see that I can provide more than you'll ever need? Why do you turn inward and kick yourself? Turn to me!"

When he fed the five thousand Jesus got upset because people tried to control him. Now he's upset that the disciples are distant from him. In the first instance the people have a wrong kind of faith. Now the disciples evidence an absence of faith. Faith is not some kind of spiritual energy. It's realizing that we don't have the resources for living. It's turning to Jesus and saying, "I have no bread. I have no wine. I have no love." It's joining the tax collector in the temple, saying, *"God be merciful to me a sinner.* I can't do life on my own anymore." <u>Faith goes to God with our weakness</u>, just as Jesus wanted his disciples to come to him. That connection solves real problems—like forgetting to bring bread. Or not being able to love your mom or your roommate.

Jesus wants his disciples to do what the outcasts and the sick have been doing. Zacchaeus climbed a tree in order to see Jesus. The bleeding woman pushed her way through the crowd and reached out to touch Jesus. When people told blind Bartimaeus to be quiet, *he shouted all the more, "Son of David, have mercy on me!"* (Mark 10:48). Another group of guys pulled the shingles off a roof to lower their sick friend to Jesus (Mark 2:4). <u>Jesus wants people to move toward him in faith</u>, just as he has been moving toward them in love. Again and again, he tells these people, *"Your faith has healed you.* Your willingness to come to me empty-handed, without an agenda, is the door to me helping you."

That is a hard move to make if your hands are full. A young, wealthy man comes to Jesus and asks him what he needs to do to get eternal life. When Jesus tells him to obey the Ten Commandments he replies, *"All these I have kept since I was a boy." Jesus looked at him and loved him (Mark 10:20-21).* Jesus' heart is drawn toward this genuinely good man. Then Jesus acts to help him, telling him he has one more thing to do: *"Go, sell everything you have and give to the poor, and you will have treasure in heaven. Then come, follow me"* (10:21). Jesus offers him freedom from the bondage of money, and he offers a new center to the man's life. But the man is captive to the false security and easy gratification that money brings, so *he went away sad, because he had great wealth* (10:22). Jesus looks, feels, and offers help, but when the man rejects Jesus' help, Jesus does nothing. He lets him go. Jesus is not trapped by his own compassion nor is he driven to rescue this wealthy but sad man.

The Feel of Faith

C. S. Lewis captures what faith feels like in a children's story. A schoolgirl named Jill Pole goes to a stream to drink, but at the side of the stream lies a large lion. She stops. The lion tells her, "If you're thirsty, you may drink." Jill hesitates.

> "Are you not thirsty?" said the Lion.
>
> "I'm *dying* of thirst," said Jill.
>
> "Then drink," said the Lion.
>
> "May I—could I—would you mind going away while I do?" said Jill.
>
> The Lion answered this only by a look and a very low growl. . . .
>
> "Will you promise not to—do anything to me if I do come?" said Jill.
>
> "I make no promise," said the Lion. . . .
>
> "Do you eat girls?" she said.
>
> "I have swallowed up girls and boys, women and men, kings and emperors, cities and realms," said the Lion. It didn't say this as if it were boasting, nor as if it were sorry, nor as if it were angry. It just said it.
>
> "I daren't come and drink," said Jill.
>
> "Then you will die of thirst," said the Lion.
>
> "Oh dear!" said Jill, coming another step nearer. "I must go and look for another stream, then."
>
> "There is no other stream," said the Lion.[2]

In this allegorical story, Jill represents us and the Lion symbolizes Jesus. Like Jill, we are drawn by the fresh water of the stream, but we fear the Lion. We don't want to lose control of our lives, yet we want to drink. We don't want to appear foolish, becoming a "religious nut," yet our lives don't work. Our feelings about Jesus are mixed.

At the Feast of the Tabernacles, the most joyous of the feasts,

178

the Jews brought up water from the pool of Siloam and poured it out. The water symbolized the pouring out of God's love when the Messiah would come. During the feast, Jesus got up in the temple and made an unabashed claim to be the solution for our deepest thirsts. *"If anyone is thirsty, let him come to me and drink. Whoever believes in me, as the Scripture has said, streams of living water will flow from within him"* (John 7:37-38).

How Does Faith Work in Day-to-Day Living?

One year I took five of our kids camping. Jill had sworn off camping after a disaster the previous year, so she stayed home with Kim, who was eight at the time.

Within the first hour of a four-hour drive, Andrew (5) and Emily (3) were asking, "Are we there yet?" We found a lovely camping spot up a flight of wooden steps, dug out of the side of the mountain.

The first thing I discovered was that the last person who borrowed our camp stove forgot to return the connecting hose for the propane tanks. So for our first night, we cooked spaghetti over an open fire.

The older kids had put up a hammock and after a few minutes of fun began arguing. I remember setting the table, yelling at the kids while paper plates were carried off in gusts of wind. I was also keeping an eye out for Emily, who kept wandering near the fire.

Andrew was having a ball. With Mom not around, I let him use the hatchet to get wood for the fire. He kept coming back with nice pieces, until one of the older kids tattled: "Dad, he's chopping up the park service steps." After putting an end to that, we sat down for a dinner of partly burned spaghetti. Everyone was irritable.

The next day we went into town to hunt for a replacement hose. Every clerk was sure that the next store would have it. After four stores and half the day, I gave up and bought some sterno on the recommendation of a salesperson. I soon discovered that cooking with sterno is like heating a house with candles.

That night it rained. We were at the bottom of a small mountain, and we had pitched our tent in what must have been an old streambed. I went outside with a flashlight and dug a makeshift ditch around the tent, but it didn't help. Our tent was old, and it leaked if you touched the sides. To make matters worse, rain was pouring through the tent door because the zipper was broken. We partially closed it using shoelaces, but we were so tired and wet that we didn't remove them from the shoes, so the door had all these shoes dangling from it.

In the morning we were grumpy, mean, and wet to the bone. We had to do something to dry off. I decided to take a trip to another park that was supposed to be only an hour-and-a-half away. I'd turn the heater up, and we'd dry off in the car.

As it got quiet, I looked around at the kids as, one by one, exhausted and wet, they drifted off to sleep. They looked so sweet now—you'd never know how irritable and selfish they'd been. Their attitudes were the worst part of the trip. They'd been miserable. I began to worry.

Then I thought about how I'd been—impatient, barking orders, quick to criticize—and I got more nervous. I was a mess. In fact, our whole family was a mess. It took the pressure of the camping trip for me to see it. Clearly, I couldn't fix them or myself. I thought, "I need Jesus." It wasn't even a prayer; it was just a fact. Unless Jesus helped our family, we were headed for disaster.

I turned to him for help in a way I never had before.

What happened because of my faith? Did our family get less cranky? Yes. But it happened in a very surprising—and painful— way. Funny thing; Jesus didn't start working on the kids, but on me. He answered my plea, I believe, by letting me burn out that fall from too much work—work that I was doing on my own that in retrospect wasn't all that important. And Jill became less meek.

180

Rats. That was the winter she asked, "Paul, do you love me?"

On the camping trip I realized that I didn't have control. I didn't turn away from my quick, confident, advice-giving parenting just because it wasn't working. I wasn't working. That led to my desperate prayer. But even then I did not understand myself or my most basic needs. I just wanted assistance, a partner, someone to help me bail. Instead, I got a king and ended up losing more control. Jesus continues to do the unexpected.

When I prayed for help I was "doing" faith. I did both sides of faith: I realized I was needy, and I went to God with that need. Both parts equate faith. That brought love into our family.

181

CHAPTER SEVENTEEN

THE INTIMATE STRANGER

WEAVING A FABRIC OF LOVE

*U*P TILL NOW WE'VE BEEN LOOKING AT INDIVIDUAL parts of Jesus' love, but not the whole. When you first learn to drive a car you practice the parts of driving—accelerating, steering, braking—in a controlled environment. But eventually you have to go out on the road and do everything at the same time. Watch Jesus weave together the distinct patterns of his love into a beautiful fabric as he strikes up a conversation with a woman in the middle of a tiring day.

FIRST, COMPASSION

From down in the Jordan River valley, Jesus and his disciples make their way up a ravine into the land of the Samaritans, to the ancient well of Jacob. Looming over the well are two mountains, Mount Gerizim and Mount Ebal, considered sacred to the Samaritans.

Map of Mid~Palestine

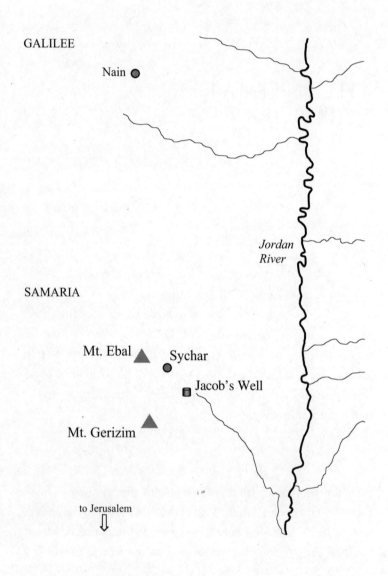

GALILEE

Nain

SAMARIA

Mt. Ebal   Sychar

Jacob's Well

Mt. Gerizim

Jordan River

to Jerusalem

At the foot of Mount Ebal lies the village of Sychar, just a half-mile from the well where Jesus sits.[1] The valley of Samaria, with its silvery olive groves, spreads out below; fields of ripening barley wave in the soft midday breeze.

> *. . . he left Judea and went back once more to Galilee.*
>
> *Now he had to go through Samaria. So he came to a town in Samaria called Sychar, near the plot of ground Jacob had given to his son Joseph. Jacob's well was there, and Jesus, tired as he was from the journey, sat down by the well. It was about the sixth hour. When a Samaritan woman came to draw water, Jesus said to her, "Will you give me a drink?" (His disciples had gone into the town to buy food.)*
>
> *The Samaritan woman said to him, "You are a Jew and I am a Samaritan woman. How can you ask me for a drink?" (For Jews do not associate with Samaritans.) (John 4:3-9)*

The journey up the ravine was hot and tiring—the eastern ridge of the Judean hills is a desert. While Jesus sits on the covering over the well, the disciples go to Sychar to get food. A woman approaches alone at midday, balancing an empty water jar on her head. That's strange—village women usually draw water together in the early evening or morning. A servant is not drawing water for her, which indicates that she's from the lower class.

That Jesus talked with her at all is astonishing. For one thing, women were second-class citizens. A woman had no recourse to legal help if her husband beat her. Her husband could divorce her simply by saying three times, "I divorce you." Jewish rabbis specifically warned against speaking with a woman in public.[2] The equivalent for us is a white person in the Deep South in 1950 sitting in the back of a bus with a black person.

For another thing, the Jews and Samaritans had a long history of hatred and hostility. The Samaritans were a Jewish subculture that held sacred only the five books of Moses and worshiped in a

185

temple they had erected on Mount Gerizim, instead of in Jerusalem. Although Samaria was between the two major centers of Jewish population—Galilee to the north and Judea to the south—some Jews would take a large detour through the Jordan River valley to avoid setting foot in Samaria. A Jewish person would not eat from a bowl that had been touched by a Samaritan.

Yet Jesus asked this Samaritan woman for a drink, giving her dignity and respect. She recognizes his ethnic background either from his Galilean accent or the blue fringes on his garment (the Samaritans had yellow fringes). A typical village woman who was spoken to by a rabbi in public would quietly draw water, give him the drink without making eye contact, and then return to the village to tell her friends. But not her. She throws up the differences between them—something people are shy to do even today with a complete stranger. Shocked, she reacts: "How can you ask me for a drink? Don't you understand you're not supposed to talk to a Samaritan woman in public? Aren't you supposed to hate me? What planet are you from?" She is direct, bold, and a little brassy.

Jesus is bold and direct in return:

> Jesus answered her, "If you knew the gift of God and who it is that asks you for a drink, you would have asked him and he would have given you living water."
>
> "Sir," the woman said, "you have nothing to draw with and the well is deep. Where can you get this living water? Are you greater than our father Jacob, who gave us the well and drank from it himself, as did also his sons and his flocks and herds?" (John 4:10-12)

Jesus' intriguing way of answering her fits her direct style. He repeatedly invites her to come on strong. He's in her face, bantering with her. Notice how they bounce the word *you* back and forth. Jesus speaks her language as he piques her interest with the suggestion that he could give her *living water*. Her reply continues the

LOVE WALKED AMONG US

game, sending the word *you* back into his court: "Right, what else are *you* going to tell me? Do *you* think *you* are a bigger deal than Jacob?"

In the face of her challenge, Jesus continues to intrigue her by hinting at what he means by living water. *Jesus answered, "Everyone who drinks this water will be thirsty again, but whoever drinks the water I give him will never thirst. Indeed, the water I give him will become in him a spring of water welling up to eternal life"* (4:13-14). He tells her that he has something that will meet a need deeper than the need for water. As we'll see in a moment, this woman has tried to satisfy the thirst of her soul with men—and it hasn't worked. What the Jews were trying to find in a political Messiah, she has been trying to find in men. She has kept coming back to the same old well again and again, only to come up empty.

But now she "calls his cards." *The woman said to him, "Sir, give me this water so that I won't get thirsty and have to keep coming here to draw water"* (4:15). Her hands are on her hips as she looks him in the eye. What on earth is he talking about?

THEN, HONESTY

This woman has been married five times, and she is not married to the man she is living with now. Jesus tells her: *"Go, call your husband and come back."* Jesus is deadly serious, and she feels it.

She shuts the door with a terse reply: *"I have no husband"* (4:16-17)—four words compared with an earlier average of thirty-two. She goes from being absolutely frank to completely hidden. "It was nice talking, but I am no longer enjoying this." End of conversation. But Jesus keeps invading her life with his honesty. *Jesus said to her, "You are right when you say you have no husband. The fact is, you have had five husbands, and the man you now have is not your husband. What you have just said is quite true"* (4:17-18).

First, Jesus exposes the dark side of her life, and then he confronts the dishonesty of her answer. He gently and persistently holds up her half-truth in front of her, underlining it three times: *"You are right . . . The fact is . . . What you have said is quite true."* Quite true—but not in the way you meant it. She has asked for water that will quench her thirst, and Jesus tells her, "How can I give you living water if you are drinking from wells that don't satisfy?" She's still thirsty because she keeps trying new wells. Jesus invites her to have faith in him, but points out that she can't if her faith is in men. Jesus loves her just the way she is, yet he refuses to leave her the way she is.

What does she do when boxed into a corner? She compliments Jesus' insight. *"Sir," the woman said, "I can see you are a prophet. Our fathers worshiped on this mountain, but you Jews claim that the place where we must worship is in Jerusalem"* (4:19-20).

This woman knows the male ego well. Buttering up worked with at least six guys, so why not try it on this one? She is both irresistible and distant, both charming and deceitful. The compliment is just a hook to begin a religious argument and distance herself from Jesus. With the Samaritan's most sacred site right behind her, taking a swipe at Jerusalem and Jewish religion seems perfect. She sends a clear message: "You have your religion, and I have mine. Don't try to change me."

She's on her feet again—her word count is back up to twenty-eight! In one swift move, she has complimented Jesus, changed the subject, and tried to start an argument.

BACK TO COMPASSION

But this is no ordinary Jewish man:

> *Jesus declared, "Believe me, woman, a time is coming when you will worship the Father neither on this mountain nor in Jerusalem. You Samaritans worship what you do not know; we worship what we do know, for salvation is from the Jews. Yet a time is coming and has now come when the true worshipers will worship the Father in spirit and truth, for they are the kind of worshipers the Father seeks.*

God is spirit, and his worshipers must worship in spirit and in truth." (John 4:21-24)

Rather than demanding that she listen to him, Jesus continues to treat her with dignity by answering her question. He calls God *Father*, and tells her that the Father is going to change all religion and that people will no longer need a specific place to worship God because everyone will have complete access to him. And yes, somehow, that complete access to the Father is going to come through the Jews. God is seeking people—like this woman—who will worship him.

Still trying to divert attention from herself, she suggests that this is a matter for the religious experts. *The woman said, "I know that Messiah" (called Christ) "is coming. When he comes, he will explain everything to us" (4:25).* In other words, "*You* can stop explaining." The fight is draining out of her. Her familiar world is in shambles. In the space of a few minutes, this master surgeon has precisely exposed her cancer and offered to heal her completely.

And he isn't finished. *Then Jesus declared, "I who speak to you am he" (4:26).* He tells this sassy, blunt, and dishonest Samaritan woman who he is. The only other time he tells someone he is the Messiah was to the high priest Caiaphas at his trial. True to form, he's again turning the established order upside down. We've seen him publicly rebuke important religious leaders and honor women and children. Jesus acts as if he has the authority to rewrite the rules.

When the disciples return, they're so surprised that Jesus is talking with a woman that their normal prejudice to Samaritans doesn't appear. *Just then his disciples returned and were surprised to find him talking with a woman. But no one asked, "What [are you seeking]?" or "Why are you talking with her?" (4:27).*[3] They notice that Jesus is *seeking* her, that he is moving toward her in love, just as the Father is *seeking* worshipers. Jesus has been gently intruding, violating her space to do her good.

The woman then leaves her water jar, goes back to the town, and coyly invites just the men with an overstatement: *"Come, see a man who told me everything I ever did. Could this be the Christ?" They came out of the town and made their way toward him* (4:28-30). She doesn't come out and say, "This is the Christ," but she raises the question, expecting the real article to sell itself to those who will come and see.

"Come meet a man who moved into my world!" she invites. "Come meet a man who saw right through me and yet accepted me! Come and meet a man who loved me just as I am! Come meet a man who showed me how empty I was! Could this be the person, promised from God, who would save us from ourselves?" The men of Sychar start pouring out of the town, coming to Jesus. (Maybe some of them are a little nervous to discover what *"everything I did"* means.) But the disciples are eyeing their lunch.

> *Meanwhile his disciples urged him, "Rabbi, eat something."*
>
> *But he said to them, "I have food to eat that you know nothing about."*
>
> *Then his disciples said to each other, "Could someone have brought him food?"*
>
> *"My food," said Jesus, "is to do the will of him who sent me and to finish his work. Do you not say, 'Four months more and then the harvest'? I tell you, open your eyes and look at the fields! They are ripe for harvest." (John 4:31-35)*

Jesus isn't hungry anymore. He is full because he has done his Father's will in loving this woman and pointing her to a deeper source of life and joy than men. Jesus has been depending on his Father, even as he has been asking the woman to depend on him. Then he sees the woman returning with men streaming after her, and tells the disciples, *"Open your eyes and look."* Look at all these people. They are the real harvest field. Here are more people to love—more worshipers for his heavenly Father.

In this encounter Jesus weaves a fabric of love. He's a stranger, yet he moves close. He's tired, yet he talks. He's a Jew, yet he cares for a Samaritan. He's a first-century man, yet he treats a peasant woman with dignity. He's serious, yet he plays. He's compassionate, yet honest. He's right, yet undemanding. He's hungry, yet full. He's unlike any person who ever existed. The more we look at him the more clearly we can see how fractured and broken we are. He is humanity as it should be.

At the Feast of Tabernacles when Jesus says, *"If anyone is thirsty, let him come to me and drink,"* the religious rulers send temple guards to arrest him. When the guards come back empty-handed, the priests ask them, *"Why didn't you [arrest him]?"* They reply, *"No one ever spoke the way this man does"* (John 7:45-46).

Napoleon had the same reaction as the guards when he began reading the Gospels in his last days on the island of Elba. He told General Bertrand,

> I know men; and I tell you that Jesus Christ is not a man. Superficial minds see a resemblance between Christ and the founders of empires and the gods of other religions. That resemblance does not exist. Everything in him astonishes me. His spirit overawes me, and his will confounds me. Between him and whoever else in the world, there is no possible term of comparison. He is truly a being by himself.[4]

CHAPTER EIGHTEEN

ONENESS

LOVE LEADS TO INTIMACY

*L*OVE IS A JOURNEY INTO JOY, A MOVEMENT TOWARD another person that results in intimacy, in oneness. Yet intimacy eludes us. It's fragile, difficult to maintain, and easy to lose. So good, but so rare.

Jesus, like most of us, had circles of friendship with ever increasing intimacy. He had an outer circle of disciples, but he spent most of his time with his twelve disciples. He was especially close to Peter, James, and John, particularly John. But his relationship with his Father expresses his deepest intimacy.

About this relationship, he said: *"For the Father loves the Son and shows him all he does"* (*John* 5:20). Jesus and his Father hide nothing from each other. They know one another completely: *". . . as the Father knows me and I know the Father . . . "* (*John* 10:15). The word "knowing," in English, means "understanding information about something." But "knowing" in Hebrew means knowing and being known: intimacy.[1] When Adam and Eve had sexual relations, the Bible says Adam "knew" Eve. You don't get this kind of knowing from a book.

The Father and the Son give to each other unreservedly. In his final prayer, Jesus tells his Father, *"All I have is yours, and all you have is mine"* (*John* 17:10). "I own nothing—I give it all to you. You own nothing—you give it all to me. Neither of us holds anything back. Our trust in each other is total." When he talks about his Father, Jesus uses the language of intimacy: "*. . . you are in me and I am in you*" (17:21). The two are one in purpose, knowledge, and affection.

The Father speaks of his love for his Son. At Jesus' baptism in the Jordan River, a voice from heaven says, *"You are my Son, whom I love"* (*Luke* 3:22). Later at a mountain in northern Israel, the Father says of Jesus, *"This is my Son, whom I love; with him I am well pleased"* (*Matthew* 17:5).

Jesus speaks to his Father with similar affection. In the Garden of Gethsemane, just before soldiers come to take him away, Jesus prays, *"Abba, Father"* (*Mark* 14:36). The Aramaic word *abba* is much like our word "daddy," except it's more reverent. Jesus' relationship with his Father was so close, so dependent, so intimate, he called God "Daddy". No one talked to God using *abba*—it was too intimate— but Jesus' intimacy with his father had such an impact on his followers that the Greek-speaking church continued to use the word *abba*.

Jesus' description of his relationship with his Father suggests this summary of oneness: Oneness is a state of pure and constant compassion devoid of selfishness. Your needs are so totally mine that "I am in you." My needs are so totally yours that "You are in me." We have no secrets—our hearts touch each other's fully. Each of us gives to the other all we have. Our joy is complete in each other.

Intimacy is a strange thing. I remember times when Jill has felt safe enough to open up her heart and share with me a hidden grief or a simple joy. That she knows I understand a hidden part of her heart is priceless. Such moments are unrepeatable; I wish I could grab and bottle them, but I can't. I can only remember them. Even if I could reproduce the moment with the exact words and circumstances, I couldn't reproduce our closeness. We can't have intimacy on demand. It happens when we love.

194

Intimacy isn't always deep or intense. At times Jill and I have felt close to each other simply by getting away together and replacing the whining of kids with the rhythmic click-clack of horses in the Amish countryside. Or, we experience closeness in moments of shared family fun, like when we finally discovered a game that Kim enjoyed playing with the rest of us. This question stumped all of us (our apologies to Rolling Rock), but was a no-brainer for Kim: "Name a beer that begins with the letter R." Kim didn't hesitate as she typed on her speaking computer, "root beer."

Intimacy grows. It takes years of compassion and honesty, and then slowly, quietly, two people can have an almost constant connection. They move from being irritated at the other's foibles to laughing at them, from distance to closeness.

A Key to Understanding the Universe

Jesus sums up his relationship with his Father this way: *"I and the Father are one"* (John 10:30). Two people can't get any closer, more intimate. When Jesus said this, the Jews were infuriated because they recognized he was claiming to be God.

> *Again, the Jews picked up stones to stone him, but Jesus said to them, "I have shown you many great miracles from the Father. For which of these do you stone me?"*
>
> *"We are not stoning you for any of these," replied the Jews, "but for blasphemy, because you, a mere man, claim to be God." (John 10:31-33)*

After Jesus' last meal with his disciples he prays, *"And now, Father, glorify me in your presence with the glory I had with you before the world began"* (John 17:5). Jesus claimed that he lived before the creation of the world. Before all else the Father was loving the Son. Jesus tells his Father, *". . . you loved me before the creation of the world"* (17:24).

195

That love was the primal pool for all else as it exploded into creation. Jesus asks his Father that *"the love you have for me may be in them"* (17:26).

The love that is at the center of the universe now extends outward through Jesus to his followers. Jesus tells his Father that he has *"loved them even as you have loved me"* (17:23). The Father "knew" Jesus. In turn, Jesus takes the time to "know" people by asking questions. He knows their failings. He knows the pain of others. He is "in" people's emotional lives and "in" their problems. He touches people. When we watch Jesus, we are watching God respond to human suffering.

Jesus prays, *"I want those you have given me to be with me where I am, and to see my glory, the glory you have given me because you loved me before the creation of the world"* (17:24). The river of his Father's love was so sweet, so beyond comprehension, that it poured through Jesus into the world. The beauty of the Father (his glory) must be shared. Love always leads to creation, to life, to hope. Jesus desires that we experience and reflect the same oneness he has with the Father. In looking at the future, he asks, *"that all of them may be one, Father, just as you are in me and I am in you. May they also be in us . . . that they may be one as we are one: I in them and you in me"* (17:21-23).

Love expands like ripples in a pond, moving ever outward from the Father to Jesus, from Jesus to his followers, and from them to us. We see these ripples when Jesus tells Zacchaeus, *"I'm going to your house today,"* or when he tells the Samaritan woman, *"Give me a drink."*

Jesus said that when people look at his followers, they should be able to see him: *"By this all men will know that you are my disciples, if you love one another"* (John 13:35). He also said that we could look through him to the Father. When Philip asks Jesus, *"Show us the Father and that will be enough for us,"* Jesus replies, *"Don't you know me, Philip, even after I have been among you such a long time? Anyone who has seen me has seen the Father"* (John 14:8-9). If you've seen Jesus, you've seen God.

Why Isn't There More Love?

If love is at the center of the universe, why is there so much conflict, hatred, fear, and disillusionment in the world? Why isn't there more love?

To answer this question, think about how love works. We choose whether we will receive and give love. We aren't robots. Jean-Paul Sartre observes:

> The man who wants to be loved does not desire the enslavement of his beloved. He is not bent on becoming the object of passion, which flows forth mechanically. He does not want to possess an automaton, and if we want to humiliate him, we need try to only persuade him that the beloved's passion is the result of psychological determinism. The lover will feel that both his love and his being are cheapened. . . . If the beloved is transformed into an automaton, the lover finds himself alone.[2]

We must be able to accept or reject love—otherwise it's not love, just computer programming. When God created people who could love, he created people who could reject him, who could take their ability to love and use it to act independently of God. The father, in the parable of the Lost Son, lets his son go, giving him the freedom to reject his love.[3]

When we do our own thing instead of trusting God, we become separated from him and one another. The world becomes broken. The possibility of love creates the possibility of separation and, ultimately, evil. Scripture traces how Adam and Eve, faced with choosing between loving God or becoming independent, chose self-willed independence. The nature of God dictates the nature of love and the nature of people.

God has called his human children to form a great circle where we all stand, arms linked together, facing toward the light in the center, which is God himself. We should see our fellow creatures standing around that central love that shines on us and illuminates our faces, and join with them in the dance of God, the rhythm of love. But instead of choosing to face the center, we have turned our backs on God and each other, and face the other way so that we can neither see the light at the center nor the faces in the circle. Instead of enjoying God and each other, we play our own selfish little game, each one wanting to be the center. No longer do we understand God or ourselves. The light of God still shines from the true center upon our backs, though not on our faces. Because we were created for something better, we are dimly aware that all is not well. We don't feel our separation from God but we feel its effects—a sense of deadness, of alienation, of profound loneliness, of cosmic emptiness.[4]

How can God include us in the circle of his love if we are committed to self? He can't. Self rules instead of love. Sin—stubborn self-will and self-seeking—destroys oneness. Without God's love to satisfy us, we try to fill the hole in our lives with happy vacations, new lovers, work, and children. But with each one we come away empty. Our longing tells us that we were designed for something better. We long to return to the circle of the Father's love. We long for the very thing that eludes us. That's what Isabelle's mother did.

Isabelle's father raped her when she was a child. When she confronted her father as an adult, her mother shut her daughter out of her life, refusing to communicate with her in any way. But Isabelle began to give her mom small tokens of love. She sent her birthday cards, notes on holidays, and small gifts. Finally, after ten years, her mother responded. She told her daughter, "I've treated you so badly and you have continued to love me. I've so wanted to reach out to you, but I just couldn't."

Her words, "but I just couldn't," capture the paradox of intimacy. We long deeply for something that we violently spurn. Isabelle's mom longed to reach out to her daughter, but she just couldn't.

LOVE WALKED AMONG US

She was the center of her own circle, her own world. Her pride kept her from getting close to her daughter. The two problems— distance from God and one another—are inseparable.

Jesus believed that he came to restore the ancient union with God and people. Until now, we've seen Jesus love people as he encounters them. The gospel writers suggest that in his death, Jesus' love embraces the entire world. The plot for his death begins when the Jewish leaders assemble the Sanhedrin. They fear that Jesus will lead a rebellion against the Romans, who would retaliate by destroying Israel. Caiaphas, the high priest, takes the mike.

> *"You do not realize that it is better for you that one man die for the people than that the whole nation perish."*
>
> *He did not say this on his own, but as high priest that year he prophesied that Jesus would die for the Jewish nation, and not only for that nation but also for the scattered children of God, to bring them together and make them one. So from that day on they plotted to take his life. (John 11:50-53)*

Jesus died to bring people *together and make them one*. The goal of his love is oneness. By "dying" to natural Jewish male prejudices, he becomes one with the Samaritan woman at the well. By dying on the cross, he restores oneness to all *the scattered children of God*. In the last part of this book, we'll see how that works.

Returning to Joy

When oneness is restored, joy returns. The angel tells the shepherds at Jesus' birth, *"I bring you good news of great joy that will be for all the people"* (Luke 2:10). His very arrival brings joy.

The joy at his arrival set the tone for his life. Jesus enjoyed himself so much that he was accused of being *"a glutton and a drunkard"* (*Matthew 11:19*). We often see him at banquets or feasts. A first-century banquet was like a good party, sometimes lasting for days. The prophet Zechariah said that when the Messiah would come, the fasts would turn into feasts (Zechariah 8:19).[5] When asked why his disciples don't fast, he said, *"How can the guests of the bridegroom fast while he is with them?"* (*Mark* 2:19). The very presence of Jesus is reason enough for a party.

Jesus went out of his way to celebrate with the outcasts of society. Jesus' partying with low-lifes bugged the ever-alert Pharisees, who complained, *"Why do you eat and drink with tax collectors and 'sinners'?"* Jesus replied, *"It is not the healthy who need a doctor, but the sick. I have not come to call the righteous, but sinners to repentance"* (*Luke* 5:30-31). Jesus finds joy in restoring people to the sanity of a God-centered life.

As we saw in chapter two, the lost son realized he'd been crazy to leave his father's house. He came to his senses and returned home to find his father eagerly looking for him. His father tells the servants: *"Quick! Bring the best robe and put it on him. Put a ring on his finger and sandals on his feet. Bring the fattened calf and kill it. Let's have a feast and celebrate. For this son of mine was dead and is alive again; he was lost and is found"* (*Luke* 15:17,22-24). When the father orders the calf slaughtered, he invites the whole town to come to the party. Otherwise, he would have wasted the meat (they didn't have refrigerators back then) and insulted the town.[6] The father is so full of joy he can't help but throw a huge party.

When the stay-at-home, holier-than-thou, older brother expresses his disgust at this, his father pleads: *"We had to celebrate and be glad, because this brother of yours was dead and is alive again; he was lost and is found"* (15:31-32). The lost son has reentered the circle of the father's love, the circle of joy. He has come home, and tastes what Jesus has tasted from the beginning of time.

The son turned his back on his father and tried to create his own joy by spending his father's money. Likewise, our culture tells us that getting—being rich or good-looking or popular—brings joy, but it doesn't. Like the son, we soon discover that when we reach the goal, we are empty. The joy is fleeting. Like the father, Jesus'

200

joy is so big that he tells his disciples that he wants them to *"have the full measure of my joy"* (John 17:13). His joy is a possession (*"my joy"*), a constant, steady presence in the center of his personality. We get this joy, not by working at it or creating it through human experience, but by returning to the father, by resting in God's love for us. Jesus also told his disciples: *"As the Father has loved me, so have I loved you. Now remain in my love. . . . I have told you this so that my joy may be in you and that your joy may be complete"* (John 15:9,11). Jesus is the door to his Father's joy. To experience his love is to possess joy.

Isabelle was able to move toward her mom when most people would have told her that she had every reason to write her off. It seemed crazy to reach out to her mom. Her mom had cut her off simply because Isabelle was honest about evil in their home. What freed Isabelle to love her "enemy"? Isabelle realized that she had the same problem as her mother—a determination to live a self-centered life instead of a God-centered life. She saw her mom as a fellow struggler. When Isabelle turned around and faced the center of the circle, she could love her mom. God gave her the power to love.

Isabelle said that the happiest day of her life was when she got the letter of apology from her mom. The hard work of love had led to intimacy, which bubbled over into joy. Joy comes not only from resting in God's love for us, but also in showing love to others. Jesus told his disciples that when they would *"love each other as I have loved you,"* then their joy would be complete (John 15:11-12).

If Isabelle had tried to "do" intimacy, she would have messed up. Her mom would have felt pressure instead of love. She wouldn't have left any space for her mom to change. Intimacy isn't something we "do"; it just happens when we love.

Jesus became alone so that we
wouldn't have to be alone.

Be

PART 5
LOVE MOVES
THROUGH
DEATH
INTO LIFE

CHAPTER NINETEEN

THE WAY OF HUMILITY

LOVE TAKES THE LOWER PLACE

ENRI NOUWEN WAS AT THE TOP OF HIS profession:

Everyone was saying I was doing really well, but something inside me was telling me that my success was putting my soul in danger. I found myself praying poorly, living somewhat isolated from other people, and very much preoccupied with burning issues. I woke up one day with the realization that I was living in a very dark place.

In the midst of this I kept praying, "Lord, show me where you want me to go and I will follow you, but please be clear and unambiguous about it!" Well, God was. In the person of Jean Vanier, the founder of L'Arche communities for mentally handicapped people, God said, "Go and live among the poor in spirit, and they will heal you." So I moved from Harvard to L'Arche, from the best and the brightest, wanting to rule the world, to men and woman who had few or no words and were considered, at best, marginal to the needs of our society. It was a very hard and painful move.[1]

Nouwen left a successful and prestigious career to care for disabled adults. In order to love the disabled, he had to go where they were. To do that, he had to leave where he was. He humbled himself. He had to go low in order to love. Love and humility are inseparable.

Love isn't a one-shot sortie into someone else's need. It gets involved; it doesn't stay clean and separate. In this last part of the book, we will examine the cost of Jesus' love. The Gospels trace in great detail his final journey to death, how he loved, and what he felt.

Who Is the Greatest?

As Jesus gets closer to his death, his disciples exalt themselves. However, there is only so much room at the top. Several fights break out on their way to Jerusalem. In three different incidents, the disciples grab for power. Each time Jesus brings them down.

After a brief retreat with Peter, James, and John, Jesus returns to find the other nine disciples frustrated that they can't perform a miracle. It is a perfect formula for a fight: three guys get promoted and nine muck up the job. While on the road south, the disciples argue:

> *They came to Capernaum. When he was in the house, he asked them, "What were you arguing about on the road?" But they kept quiet because on the way they had argued about who was the greatest.*
>
> *Sitting down, Jesus called the Twelve and said, "If anyone wants to be first, he must be the very last, and the servant of all."*
>
> *He called a little child and had him stand among them. And he said: "I tell you the truth, unless you change and become like little children, you will never enter the kingdom of heaven. Therefore,*

whoever humbles himself like this child is the greatest in the kingdom of heaven. And whoever welcomes a little child like this in my name welcomes me." (Mark 9:33-35; Matthew 18:2-5)

Archaeologists believe they have uncovered Peter's home in Capernaum: a small fisherman's house near the shore of Galilee.[2] Picture the disciples crowded into a small living area, shuffling their feet and staring out the window as Jesus quizzes them. Very tenderly, he takes a little child, a boy, and holds him up as an example. It wasn't that the child was pure—that is a modern idea that would have seemed strange in the first century. In Jesus' day a child was at the absolute bottom of the pecking order. He was the lowest of the low, a perfect example of humility, weakness, and need. Jesus once again turns things upside down and says that the person in the lowest place—the humble person—is the greatest.

The second time occurred when James and John used their mother to try to get the top jobs in Jesus' kingdom. Jesus gently deflates their ambition.

> *"You don't know what you are asking," Jesus said to them. "Can you drink the cup I am going to drink?"*
>
> *"We can," they answered.*
>
> *Jesus said to them, "You will indeed drink from my cup. . . ."*
>
> *When the ten heard about this, they were indignant with the two brothers. Jesus called them together and said, "You know that the rulers of the Gentiles lord it over them, and their high officials exercise authority over them. Not so with you. Instead, whoever wants to become great among you must be your servant, and whoever wants to be first must be your slave —just as the Son of Man did not come to be served, but to serve, and to give his life as a ransom for many." (Matthew 20:22-28)*

When the other ten disciples get wind of this power play, they are steaming. But just as he doesn't with James and John, Jesus doesn't react to the disciples' egos—possibly because the disciples are so upfront, unlike the Pharisees.

Jesus calls the disciples together and tells them that their whole approach to life is wrong. He invites them to a life of compassion and service instead of a pursuit of power and fame, again reversing everything humans instinctively cherish. Nouwen reflects on why we pursue power over love:

> What makes the temptation to power so seemingly irresistible? Maybe it is that power offers an easy substitute for the hard task of love. It seems easier to be God than to love God, easier to control people than to love people, easier to own life than to love life.[3]

Jesus' initial question to James and John, *"Can you drink the cup I am going to drink?,"* deliberately connects love with suffering instead of power. He uses an image that came from the Old Testament prophets. When Israel sinned, they "drank the cup of God's wrath." By drinking the cup of his Father's wrath, Jesus satisfies the justice of God. Jesus will compassionately take on himself the justice we deserve. His death will serve all people. He came to *give his life as a ransom for many.* In contrast to their desire to gain life through power, Jesus loses his life because of love.

The third time Jesus instructs the disciples in humility is at the Last Supper. The evening before his death, at their final meal together, the disciples again argue over who is the greatest.

> *Also a dispute arose among them as to which of them was considered to be greatest. Jesus said to them, "The kings of the Gentiles lord it over them; and those who exercise authority over them call themselves*

LOVE WALKED AMONG US

Benefactors. But you are not to be like that. Instead, the greatest
among you should be like the youngest, and the one who rules like
the one who serves. For who is greater, the one who is at the table
or the one who serves? Is it not the one who is at the table? But I am
among you as one who serves."

So he got up from the meal, took off his outer clothing, and
wrapped a towel around his waist. After that, he poured water into a
basin and began to wash his disciples' feet, drying them with the towel
that was wrapped around him. (Luke 22:24-27; John 13:4-5)

An argument over who gets the best seat might be behind this
spat. We know that Peter, the acknowledged leader of the Twelve,
would most likely be seated on Jesus' left, but instead he is so far
from Jesus that he has to whisper to John to pass a message to Jesus;
and, surprisingly, Judas appears to be very close to Jesus (John
13:24,26). Picture this scenario: Judas and Peter fighting over the
seat of honor on Jesus' left; Jesus rebuking them; then Peter, greatly
chastened, impetuously (and maybe a little dramatically) taking the
lowest seat, furthest from Jesus.

Whatever the cause of Peter's place at the Last Supper, his position
gives a sense of why we're allergic to the lower place. In order to get a
message to Jesus, he has to go through someone else. When we are at
the bottom, we are dependent on others; we have less power. We get
the meat last. We don't bask in the honor of being "favored."

Once again, we see Jesus modeling what he teaches. In this culture the servant lowest on the totem pole washed the feet of guests,
but Jesus literally becomes a servant by taking the lowest place and
washing the disciples' feet. If he weren't humble, he wouldn't have
been able to do this act of love.

Acts of love require a humble posture. When I used to help Kim
dress, I often dropped to my knees so I could match her height.
When we scrub the toilet, we kneel; when we take out the trash,
we bend our backs. People who think they're important don't take

209

the lowest place—they want the place of honor. As Jesus kneels before each man, he gives us a picture of a life devoted to love.

The Lower Place

When you're in the lowest place, people don't listen to you. They often don't take time with you, because they don't think you can give them much. They walk over you. They don't thank you. In the lowest place you may be used, overlooked, or discounted. You feel invisible.

People take the lowest place for one of two reasons. Either others chose it for us or we chose if for ourselves. When others have forced us to take the lower place, we are humiliated:

Someone dismisses our feelings, saying, "Oh, you are just being touchy."

Someone criticizes us regularly.

Someone publicly mocks us.

We are excluded from a group or a meeting.

But when we choose to take the lower place, we express humility:

We don't explain ourselves because to do so would hurt someone else.

We forgive someone rather than making an issue of it.

We give to someone in a way that no one will ever know.

Humility is a quality of the soul, something we do from inside.

Humiliation is the situation where we learn humility.

Taking the Lowest Place

We glamorize the cross as a religious symbol, but it was a disgusting and brutal instrument of death by slow torture. It was the electric chair, the hangman's noose, the syringe used for lethal injection. It was a statement from the Romans to all their conquered people: "We are the master race. You are scum."

About his coming death, Jesus said: *"The reason my Father loves me is that I lay down my life—only to take it up again. No one takes it from me, but I lay it down of my own accord"* (John 10:17-18).

These words don't seem to ring true with the circumstances surrounding Jesus' death. Others took his life—he didn't lay it down. Wasn't he going to be killed by the Romans after the Jewish leadership condemned him? Didn't the Jewish leaders demand that Pilate crucify him? Yes, but Jesus had eluded death a half-dozen times before Judas' betrayal. At the end of his life, he goes out of his way to offer himself up to the soldiers. He even encourages Judas to get moving at the Last Supper. After Jesus hands him the bread, he tells him, *"What you are about to do, do quickly"* (John 13:27). Jesus chose the lower place.

That's what love does. It takes the lower place. Here's how:

Situation: Husband tosses his underwear on the bedroom floor each morning. He's never made the connection between clean underwear and the activity of picking it up and washing it. Mom always picked it up for him at home. Wife doesn't.

Husband: "Honey, I'm all out of clean underwear."

Wife: "Can you remember to put it in the laundry basket? That way I won't forget it."

Husband: "What good would that do? You don't do the laundry anyway."

Notice how the husband shifted the conversation from him to her. Why? He's trying to win, to take the high place. The husband is clearly selfish, but to understand what humility means, let's look only at the wife. What are her options (other than dumping the laundry basket on his head)?

The typical response is retaliation: "I can't believe you said that! You're the one with the dirty laundry. I'm the one who does all the work around here." Tit for tat. But where does this lead? To more fighting, more arguing, more words—lots of words going nowhere

211

except into memory banks. When our goal is to get the other person to see our point of view, we argue. Honesty without humility doesn't work. The longer we are with someone, the more we see his or her failings. Soon we are most honest about what we don't like about each other. Retaliation just doesn't work.

But other options seem galling and unnatural:

1. Try to understand: "What do you mean when you say, 'You don't do the laundry?'"
2. Confess: "Yes, it's true that sometimes I am slow with the laundry."
3. Defend yourself without barbs: "I don't think that is true."
4. Silence (say nothing).

These responses entail stopping in the middle of the argument, and either letting the husband have the last word or admitting that he might be partly right. But isn't the husband the one with the problem? We balk at the injustice of it all. For example, let's says he's partially right. They've divided up the household chores, and she's behind on the laundry. To humbly admit that she did something wrong feels to her as if she is helping him hurt her. The argument shifts from his problem to hers, and he wins. She gives him the best seat at the table. Humility hurts, but such is love. When love is difficult, it's often because it involves humiliation.

When we choose humility during an argument, the disagreement ceases because only one person is arguing. The argument dies for want of fuel. Choosing humility doesn't necessarily mean picking up the dirty underwear or agreeing with the husband's point of view. It simply means that, rather than be controlled by the last mean thing the other person said, we take the lower place.

When we humble ourselves we create a vacuum, which God can step into and fill, rather than trying to manage and control things on our own. Jesus said, *"He who humbles himself will be exalted"*

(*Luke 14:11*). Waiting for God is the hard part.

We need faith to believe that God will take care of us when others don't. That's why we can't love without faith. All Jesus' commands assume that we will trust God. Each one asks us to go out on a limb. For instance, *"Give, and it will be given to you"* (*Luke 6:38*) requires us to stop trusting in our own resources and wait for God to provide once we've emptied our pockets.

We can't fake humility. It's so foreign to us that it takes the very energy of God. Because Jesus depends on his Father, he doesn't need to depend on his position. When we depend on God, we don't either. Faith frees us to be humble.

When we take the low place, we see clearly. Pride doesn't even notice humility, because humility is so quiet. But down low, you see not only other people better, but also yourself—and God— better. That's why the outcasts of society—children, women, foreigners, the poor and disabled—are attracted to Jesus. They see him clearly. They know they have nothing to put on the table; they are empty. Drawn by his beauty, they cling to his love.

Why Take the Low Place?

Jesus is drawn to people who are in the low place. He loves those at the bottom. Why? Because that's where he is. He said, *"Learn from me, for I am gentle and humble in heart, and you will find rest for your souls"* (*Matthew 11:29*). His first bed was a feeding trough. He ate with prostitutes and tax collectors. He talked with Samaritans. He touched lepers. His people rejected him. He died as a criminal. Jesus' heart is humble.

An alert Jew would recognize that Jesus' description of himself was how the prophets described what God was like: *"I live in a high and holy place, but also with him who is contrite and lowly in spirit"* (*Isaiah 57:15*). We can feel safe in the low place because God lives there. God is there ahead of us, inviting us to come live with him, to taste his goodness. The closest thing to the feel of God is to humble yourself, to be concerned not with position, but with people. Mother Teresa said, "The surest way to be one with God is to accept humiliation."[4]

When Jesus invites people to love, he invites them to the low place.

Ego—the self—gets in the way of love. Almost every religion recognizes this. Buddha solved the problem of self by proposing the annihilation or immersion of the self into "the all." But in getting rid of self-will, Buddhism destroys the self rather than the will.

Jesus' death is a pattern for the destruction of self-will. Just thirty years after Jesus' death, Paul told the church of Philippi,

> *Your attitude should be the same as that of Christ Jesus:*
> *Who, being in very nature God,*
> > *did not consider equality with God something to be grasped,*
> > *but made himself nothing,*
> > *taking the very nature of a servant,*
> > *being made in human likeness.*
> *And being found in appearance as a man,*
> > *he humbled himself*
> > *and became obedient to death—even death on a cross!*
> *(Philippians 2:5-8)*

To go with Jesus to his death is to die with him, to die to self. Let's go now, and walk with Jesus to the cross.

LOVE WALKED AMONG US

Chapter Twenty

FACING SADNESS

When Love Leads to Grief

EJECTION DISORIENTS US. WE GET ANGRY AT THE person who wrote us off, but wonder what is wrong with us. Often we feel a combination of hurt, anger, and depression. Even worse, betrayal adds broken intimacy and deceit to all the pain and confusion of rejection. It doesn't put just a single relationship in doubt, but our whole ability to relate, confusing us to the point of insanity.

Jesus was no stranger to rejection and betrayal. He knows what it feels like to be misunderstood and betrayed by those closest to you.

Facing Rejection from People You Love

Jesus loved the leaders of Israel and longed for closeness with Israel, but the leaders detested him. His compassion ignored their religious rules. His honesty publicly shamed them, and his oneness with his Father implied a claim to deity, which enraged them.

Jesus spoke openly about their rejection:

"O Jerusalem, Jerusalem, you who kill the prophets and stone those sent to you, how often I have longed to gather your children together, as a hen gathers her chicks under her wings, but you were not willing!" (Luke 13:34)

When danger threatens, little chicks scurry under their mother's wings. In a fire, hens will be burned alive, while their chicks are safe under their wings. Jesus wanted Israel to come to him like a chick to its mother. In the face of their rejection, he doesn't say, "Oh well, that didn't work out." He isn't a plastic Messiah—he grieves over their rejection of him and expresses his sadness as a lament, a cry of the soul.

C. S. Lewis reflected on the nature of love:

> There is no safe investment. To love at all is to be vulnerable. Love anything and your heart will be wrung and possibly broken. If you want to be sure of keeping it intact, you must give your heart to no one, not even to an animal. Wrap it carefully round with hobbies and little luxuries; avoid all entanglements; lock it up safe in the casket or coffin of your selfishness. But in that casket—safe, dark, motionless, airless—it will change. It will not be broken; it will become unbreakable, impenetrable, irredeemable. . . . The only place outside of Heaven where you can be perfectly safe from all the dangers and perturbations of love is Hell.[1]

To love is to suffer. To journey through love is to journey though sadness.

Months later, Jesus approaches Jerusalem like a conquering king.[2] After traveling up the Jericho road from the Jordan Valley, he comes over the Mount of Olives and is greeted by crowds of followers lining the sides of the road waving palm branches, the symbol

LOVE WALKED AMONG US

of military victory. As he rides on a donkey down the Mount of Olives, he sees Jerusalem spread out before him. The sight breaks his heart:

> As he approached Jerusalem and saw the city, he wept over it and said, "If you, even you, had only known on this day what would bring you peace—but now it is hidden from your eyes. The days will come upon you when your enemies will build an embankment against you and encircle you and hem you in on every side. They will dash you to the ground, you and the children within your walls. They will not leave one stone on another, because you did not recognize the time of God's coming to you." (Luke 19:41-44)

In the midst of his cheering followers, Jesus begins to weep. These aren't silent tears. What had earlier been a lament now becomes a wail. Most of us would find it uncomfortable to have been around Jesus as he poured his heart out in anguished wailing.

The crowd wants to *bring peace* by means of a human king who will destroy the Romans. Jesus wants to *bring peace* as a divine king by means of a love that dies for its enemies. Because they don't understand Jesus' real purpose, they confuse it with their own. They didn't recognize *the time of God's coming* to them in Jesus. The one who brings peace through love is *hidden from their eyes*. This devastates Jesus.

He grieves that Israel will not listen to his warning of danger to come. It didn't take a genius to predict that Israel was on a collision course with Rome. Forty years later, the Roman General Titus would have the same view of Jerusalem from the Mount of Olives. Only he wouldn't be weeping, he'd be directing his catapults.[3]

Jesus knows that in just a few days "Jerusalem" will murder him. But instead of weeping for himself, he weeps for "Jerusalem." Sadness can easily teeter into self-pity and self-absorption, but Jesus' sadness is other-centered.

217

Facing Betrayal from a Close Friend

The religious leaders have decided to put Jesus to death. But throngs of devoted followers surround Jesus during the day. In the evening when the crowds dissipated *Jesus hid himself, slipping away from the temple grounds (John 8:59)*. So the only way to get at Jesus is to get to one of his close friends. When Judas comes to them, they see their opportunity.

Judas was the disciples' treasurer. In the few glimpses we have of him, he emerges as a quiet but passionate leader who loves money. We don't know why he cracked; such is often the case with evil. But we do know when he cracked. Remember how judgmental Judas was when Martha's sister, Mary, poured perfume on Jesus? He felt that Mary's love was too extravagant, wasteful. Likely, he was genuinely disturbed by her lavish gift, and that Jesus seemed oblivious to the waste.

Jesus' sharp rebuke only made it worse. *"Leave her alone," Jesus replied. "It was intended that she should save this perfume for the day of my burial"* (John 12:7). Jesus' honesty so angers Judas, he immediately goes to the chief priests and offers to betray Jesus—for money.

Most likely, Judas had finally come to grips with Jesus' repeated insistence that he was not a human king. Deeply disappointed that Jesus is not a political Messiah who will also propel him to power, Judas is left with his bitterness and the chance to make a few bucks. Love has turned into hate. His betrayal of Jesus sets in motion a chain of events that leads to Jesus' death.

Several evenings later at their last meal together, Jesus prepares the disciples for the shock of Judas' betrayal by quoting the Old Testament: *"He who shares my bread has lifted up his heel against me"* (John 13:18). Judas had eaten, slept, and worked side-by-side with Jesus for three years. The thought of what Judas was about to do made Jesus tense. *"After he had said this, Jesus was troubled in spirit and testified, 'I tell you the truth, one of you is going to betray me'"* (13:21). The expression *troubled in spirit* means to "be agitated or restless." Jesus

LOVE WALKED AMONG US

doesn't say he's *troubled in spirit*, John just sensed it. Lying to the right of Jesus, he felt his anxiety. Jesus is not a robot, calmly saying, "Oh well, this will soon be over." He hurts.

Most of us get angry when we are hurt, and sad when we see others hurt. But Jesus is just the opposite. When he is hurt, he feels sad; when others are hurt, he gets mad. Because he is bound to the Father and not to his own feelings, he feels no bitterness or self-pity. Jesus showed us what to "do" with an enemy in chapter 10; now he shows us what to "feel." Outwardly, we are to love. Inwardly, we are to feel sadness. Anger can be a demand for immediate justice, while sadness makes no demands on the other person to be different. Sadness is a pure response to evil.

FACING DEATH

In chapter 13 we looked at how Jesus did not give in to the temptation to escape the suffering and pain of the cross. At Gethsemane Jesus is horrified at the thought of his death, because on the cross he will "drink the cup of his Father's wrath" as a payment for sin.

Six months before his death, Jesus describes his anxiety: *"But I have a baptism to undergo, and how distressed I am until it is completed!"* (*Luke 12:50*). *Baptism* is a metaphor for death. Jesus, tense and preoccupied, talked openly about his anxiety, even though some people might perceive this as a weakness. But because he was safely anchored in his Father's love, he could be weak.

A week before his death, when some Greeks inquire about Jesus, Jesus stops to reflect on the meaning of his death. He talks about a seed that loses its life for the sake of the plant that it produces: *"I tell you the truth, unless a kernel of wheat falls to the ground and dies, it remains only a single seed. But if it dies, it produces many seeds"* (*John 12:24*). His words refer to his own journey through death into life.

The Greeks—whose thinking shaped the ancient world—would have found Jesus' words strange. They believed that we were

219

caught in a cycle of despair: empires rose to glory and fell to ashes. A serious Greek play always ended in tragedy. Even in the best of times, suffering is just around the corner, haunting every celebration.[4]

But Jesus says that his death will produce life—resurrection—and this pattern will also be true for all who follow him: *"The man who loves his life will lose it, while the man who hates his life in this world will keep it for eternal life. Whoever serves me must follow me; and where I am, my servant also will be. My Father will honor the one who serves me"* (John 12:25-26). Followers of Jesus are not trapped in a cycle of despair; we are on a journey of hope. Love will come out of evil.

After reflecting on the meaning of his death, Jesus *feels* his death. He is aware that *his heart is troubled.* *"Now my heart is troubled, and what shall I say? 'Father, save me from this hour'? No, it was for this very reason I came to this hour. Father, glorify your name!"* (John 12:27-28). Often we don't even know we are sad because we won't let ourselves feel sad. But sadness still finds its way to the surface, maybe in depression or anger. Or we might try to suppress it by turning on the radio or telling a joke—anything, just so we don't have to feel our sadness.

Then Jesus feels like running: *". . . what shall I say? Father, save me from this hour?"* He's struggling with whether he should ask God to make his world pain-free. But Jesus is ruled by his Father, so he says, *"No, it was for this very reason I came to this hour."* In other words, "I am aware of my feelings, but I will not wallow in them." (Our culture makes feelings absolute: "Because I feel this way, I must act on it." But to be constantly swept along by your feelings is a modern form of bondage.) Finally Jesus worships, *"Father, glorify your name!"* The scene itself is a mini-death and resurrection. Jesus dies to his desires and then comes alive to the beauty of his Father.

Expressing our sad feelings frees us to love even those who

LOVE WALKED AMONG US

have hurt us. Jesus' response to suffering helped a friend of mine to love his boss. My friend Bryan was chief operating officer of a small, family-owned company. He had a good relationship with his boss/owner. His boss had even talked with him about taking over the running of the company and becoming the chief executive officer. That good relationship collapsed when Bryan went to his boss about the way he treated some of the employees. As a "self-made man," the boss wasn't used to criticism. He began to exclude Bryan from meetings and criticize him in front of the other managers, but he needed Bryan's skills to run the company, so he didn't let him go. Because of Bryan's family situation, finding a new job wasn't an option. He was trapped.

Bryan came to me for advice. He related that when his boss would put him down, he'd freeze from a confused combination of hurt and anger. When I described to him how Jesus experienced sadness, it gave him a new framework to relate to his boss. Later he described to me in detail a meeting where he began to respond differently. His boss had just criticized him again in front of the other managers. What he said wasn't true, but there was no point in getting into an open spat with his boss. Bryan remembered realizing that his boss wasn't going to change and treat him with respect. As the demand for his boss to change drained out of him, he was left with a sense of loss. He remembered what Jesus said and he thought: "It's okay to just be sad. It's okay for the seed to die." By being faithful in his work, not running, not lashing out, but quietly serving his family and his boss, he realized he was serving Jesus. It was a relief for him to just be sad. As he was sitting there, he recalled Jesus' comment, *"My Father will honor the one who serves me."* It occurred to him that "the one who made the Andromeda galaxy is going to honor me." Bryan told me that he found his heart worshiping, actually being joyous, in the middle of his sadness.

221

Jesus Models Sadness in Love

Jesus talks about the blessings of an appropriate sadness in the Sermon on the Mount: *"Blessed are those who mourn, for they will be comforted"* (*Matthew* 5:4). Bad sadness is endless, complicated by bitterness, self-pity, and denial. Good sadness is appropriate, simple, and honest. An ancient, disturbing prophecy said the Messiah would be *despised and rejected by men, a man of sorrows, and familiar with suffering* (*Isaiah* 53:3). Jesus faces the powerlessness and impotence of sadness without self-pity, anger, or revenge. Jesus doesn't shrink from love, he just feels sad.

Jesus' willingness to face sadness sets in motion a chain of events that leads to his greatest act of love: Because he faced his sadness, he didn't run. Because he didn't run, he suffered. Because he suffered, he died. Because he died—as we shall see—he took the sins of the world on himself. As Jesus moves toward his death, he shows us that sadness can be a quiet work of love.

LOVE WALKED AMONG US

CHAPTER TWENTY-ONE

A SYMPHONY OF LOVE

LOVE UNDER PRESSURE

*J*UST RECENTLY, JILL AND I WERE IN THE YARD WITH THE goats, and she said something that irritated me. I snapped at her and said something mean. I was cold and didn't want to be out there with all those goats—I wanted to go to my warm study and write about love!

It's relatively easy to love when things are going the way we want. But when the pressure mounts, most of us forget about love and think only about ourselves.

But not Jesus. The greater the pressure, the more we see his beauty. John writes about Jesus' final hours, *"Having loved his own who were in the world, he now showed them the full extent of his love"* (John 13:1).

During the last hours of Jesus' life, he's under a magnifying glass. It is the most concise, detailed, personal record that we have of anyone in antiquity.

GETHSEMANE

After the Last Supper, Jesus and the disciples walk across the Kidron Valley and up to Gethsemane, where Jesus prays. Near midnight, the torches of a company of soldiers and a delegation of priests pierce the darkness.

Judas leads the pack—he knows his master's hideaways—and identifies Jesus with his usual greeting of respect, a kiss. In response, Jesus makes one last attempt to reach Judas: *"Judas, are you betraying the Son of Man with a kiss?" (Luke 22:48).* Jesus holds a mirror to Judas' soul, penetrating his mask of goodness by exposing the truth of his actions. The next time we see Judas, he throws his thirty pieces of silver into the temple and screams, *"I have sinned. . . . I have betrayed innocent blood" (Matthew 27:4).* Then, overcome by his own evil, Judas ends his life.

But the wolf is at the door. Jesus steps out of the relative safety of the olive trees, placing his body between his disciples and the soldiers. He asks, *"Who is it you want?" "Jesus of Nazareth," they replied. "I am he," Jesus said (John 18:4-5).* The soldiers fall back, shocked by Jesus' majesty.

Jesus offers himself again while pleading for protection for his disciples: *"I told you that I am he. . . . If you are looking for me, then let these men go" (18:8).* Not a helpless victim, crushed by the wheel of history, Jesus freely offers his life.

At this point, Peter, bent on proving his loyalty, pulls his sword and lunges for Malchus, the High Priest's servant, cutting off his right ear. Jesus rebukes Peter sharply, *"Put your sword away! Shall I not drink the cup the Father has given me?" (18:11). And he touched the man's ear and healed him (Luke 22:51).*

Jesus performs a ballet of love—protecting, defending, touching, healing, rebuking—one move rapidly following the other, while those around him are pretending, running, striking, betraying, and murdering. He is as beautiful as they are ugly. The soldiers arrest him, binding the hands that just touched Malchus. The disciples flee into the night, captive to their fears.

THE JEWISH TRIAL

The soldiers take Jesus into Jerusalem to the house of Annas, the former high priest, for a preliminary interrogation. To their repeated questions, Jesus replies, *"I have spoken openly to the world . . . I always taught in synagogues or at the temple . . . I said nothing in secret. Why question me? Ask those who heard me. Surely they know what I said."* Angered by Jesus' honesty, *one of the officials nearby struck him in the face* (*John 18:20-22*).

But Jesus doesn't miss a beat. *"If I said something wrong,"* Jesus replied, *"testify as to what is wrong. But if I spoke the truth, why did you strike me?"* (*18:23*). As always, Jesus is honest. Direct. Confident. Unconcerned about others' opinions.

Meanwhile Peter has followed Jesus — at a distance. He's in the courtyard warming himself by a fire when a servant girl recognizes him, but Peter denies any association with Jesus. Others chime in, but Peter is adamant and begins to swear. Then, *as he was speaking, the rooster crowed. The Lord turned and looked straight at Peter* (*Luke 22:60-61*). Those familiar eyes pierce Peter's bravado. He flees weeping into the night.

Soon afterward the Sanhedrin is convened. When the witnesses present conflicting testimony about Jesus, Caiaphas intervenes:

> *"I charge you under oath by the living God: Tell us if you are the Christ, the Son of God."*
>
> *"Yes, it is as you say,"* Jesus replied. *"But I say to all of you: In the future you will see the Son of Man sitting at the right hand of the Mighty One and coming on the clouds of heaven."*
>
> *Then the high priest tore his clothes and said, "He has spoken blasphemy! Why do we need any more witnesses?"* (*Matthew 26:63-65*)

Just as the sun rises, they sentence Jesus to death. In a spontaneous groundswell of revulsion, they strike out at Jesus. Some spit

225

on him. They blindfold him and mock his supernatural powers as they strike him, saying, *"Prophesy! Who hit you?" (Luke 22:64)*. Jesus refuses to retaliate and remains silent.

But Roman law doesn't allow the Jews to put anyone to death, so they hand Jesus over to Pilate, the Roman prefect in Judea.

THE ROMAN TRIAL

Pilate goes outside of the Praetorium (his official residence) and hears a confusing array of charges against Jesus, but one piques his interest: *"We have found this man subverting our nation. He opposes payment of taxes to Caesar, and.claims to be Christ, a king" (Luke 23:2)*. Ironically, they have accused Jesus of being a political rebel, of wanting what he had so pointedly rejected, a human kingship.

Intrigued, Pilate retreats into the inner Praetorium and asks Jesus privately, *"Are you the king of the Jews?" (John 18:33)*. It is a cynical question, almost a joke: the Jews are under Roman rule, and Jesus is in chains.

Jesus probes Pilate's motivation. *"Is that your own idea . . . or did others talk to you about me?" (18:34)*. If Pilate asked this on his own initiative, that would reveal genuine interest on his part. If he heard it from others, then he is simply playing with Jesus.

Pilate snaps back, disgusted with the suggestion that he has a genuine interest in Jesus: *"Am I a Jew? . . . It was your people and your chief priests who handed you over to me."* He tries to regain control of the interrogation: *"What is it you have done?" (18:35)*.

Jesus senses Pilate's interest behind his vehement denial and answers his first question. "Yes, I am a king, but not as you think." He tells Pilate, *"My kingdom is not of this world. If it were, my servants would fight to prevent my arrest by the Jews. But now my kingdom is from another place" (18:36)*.

"You are a king, then!" said Pilate (18:37). He admits his interest, but cloaks it with cynicism and scorn.

LOVE WALKED AMONG US

Jesus answered, "You are right in saying I am a king. In fact, for this reason I was born, and for this I came into the world, to testify to the truth. Everyone on the side of truth listens to me" (18:37). Jesus is saying, "This is not a narrow Jewish question as you implied, Pilate. What I bring touches all people—*everyone*. In fact, Pilate, you could listen to me now and discover real truth." Jesus invites Pilate to believe in him and forsake the emptiness of this life. Seemingly unaware that his hands are tied behind his back, Jesus ignores Pilate's contempt and moves toward his heart. Jesus cares for this Jew-hating Roman who is about to condemn him to death.[1]

Pilate abruptly ends the conversation by denying the possibility of truth: *"What is truth?"* (18:38)—in front of the person who said, "I am the truth" (14:6).

Despite his contempt, Pilate tries to get Jesus off the hook by offering the Jews another prisoner to crucify—Barabbas. When that fails, he tries sending Jesus to Herod. Finally he hands Jesus over to his soldiers to be beaten with forty lashes. The barbed whips could go through to the bone, often killing a man. The soldiers mock Jesus' claim to be king by jamming a "crown" of thorns on his head and putting a purple robe on him.

Then Pilate parades the bruised and battered Jesus in front of the mob, hoping to get their sympathy so he can release Jesus. But someone in the crowd calls out the real charge, which they have not mentioned before, since it carries no weight under Roman law: *"We have a law, and according to that law he must die, because he claimed to be the Son of God."*

When Pilate heard this, he was even more afraid, and he went back inside the palace. "Where do you come from?" (John 19:7-9). Pilate is shaken to the core. He never met a man like this before. He wonders: "Is this a god in front of me?" Jesus has finally gotten to him. But Jesus will not defend himself. The prophecy from Isaiah about the Messiah says *he was led like a lamb to the slaughter, like a sheep before her shearers is silent* (Isaiah 53:7). Pilate again attempts to release Jesus, *but they* shouted, "Take him away! Take him away! Crucify him!"

"Shall I crucify your king?" Pilate asked.

"We have no king but Caesar," the chief priests answered (John 19:15).
Trapped by his love for power, Pilate washes his hands, pretending
to remove the stain of his guilt, and hands Jesus over to be crucified. The king has become a criminal.

THE CROSS

In the early morning, as Jesus carries the crossbeam through the
streets of Jerusalem, he collapses: either from tiredness and severe
blood loss or the game of Roman soldiers to tie a rope around the
crucified person's ankle and pull it for sport on the way to the crucifixion. The soldiers grab a passerby, Simon of Cyrene, to carry the
beam. With the load of the cross gone, Jesus turns to the wailing
women following him, and refers to the coming destruction of
Jerusalem, which happens forty years later, in A.D. 70. "Daughters
of Jerusalem, do not weep for me; weep for yourselves and for your children"
(Luke 23:28). He has just collapsed from exhaustion, but he's thinking about the women and their future pain. Jesus loves every person
he encounters.

The procession goes out the city gate to the rocky knoll where
they execute criminals, a final, public statement from Rome: "We
are the masters." They strip Jesus naked, pound nails into his wrists,
hoist the crossbeam up a wooden pole, and then pound a nail
through his feet.[2] With each hammer blow, Jesus prays, "Father,
forgive them, for they do not know what they are doing" (23:34). Instead
of insults and threats, Jesus loves his enemies by turning the other
cheek and forgiving them.

Pilate has one last joke, mocking both Jesus and his fellow Jews.
The soldiers put a sign over Jesus' head that reads This Is the King of
the Jews (23:38).

The priests surrounding the cross mock Jesus' supernatural powers:

LOVE WALKED AMONG US

"He saved others, but he can't save himself." They make fun of his claim to be God's unique Son: *"Come down from the cross, if you are the Son of God!"* They ridicule his childlike faith: *"He trusts in God. Let God rescue him now if he wants him, for he said, 'I am the Son of God'"* (Matthew 27:40,42-43).

The two revolutionaries being crucified with Jesus join in the taunts. But one is convicted, possibly by the sheer, silent goodness of Jesus, and rebukes his fellow: *"Don't you fear God,"* he said, *"since you are under the same sentence? We are punished justly, for we are getting what our deeds deserve. But this man has done nothing wrong."* Then he said, *"Jesus, remember me when you come into your kingdom."* This criminal senses the presence of a real king. Jesus responds with hope: *"I tell you the truth, today you will be with me in paradise"* (Luke 23:40-43).

Next he reaches out to provide for his mother. *When Jesus saw his mother there, and the disciple whom he loved standing nearby, he said to his mother, "Dear woman, here is your son,"* and to the disciple, *"Here is your mother"* (John 19:26-27). In the midst of his agony, Jesus never stops looking. He cares for his grieving mother, forgives the rough soldiers, gives hope to a dying criminal, and feels sad for weeping women. He overwhelms the evil around him with an undeterred, cancer-eating love.

A little while later Jesus cries out, *"My God, my God, why have you forsaken me?"* (Mark 15:34). Even as he faces his Father's silence, Jesus clings to his Father's words, *"My God, my God . . . "* quoting Psalm 22. Jesus is probably singing the Psalms quietly to himself. Shortly afterward, he cries out, *"I am thirsty"* (John 19:28), but the one who offered others living water receives only a sponge dipped in wine vinegar.

Jesus' sentences are getting progressively shorter. In order to breathe or speak, he has to push up on the nail with his feet, and pull on the nails through his wrists, scraping his raw back against the rough timber of the cross. He catches a breath of air and collapses again.

229

When he had finished the drink, Jesus said, "It is finished" (19:30). He had accomplished the Father's will. About three o'clock *Jesus called out with a loud voice, "Father, into your hands I commit my spirit." When he had said this, he breathed his last (Luke 23:46).* With his dying breath, he continues to hang onto his Father and his words, quoting Psalm 31. To the end his faith never wavers. When the Roman officer (centurion), *who stood there in front of Jesus, heard his cry and saw how he died, he said, "Surely this man was the Son of God"* (Mark 15:39).

CHAPTER TWENTY-TWO

HIS LIFE FOR OURS

THE COST OF LOVE

JILL LOVES LIFE IN ALL FORMS. NOT ONLY DO WE HAVE SIX kids, but we also have two dogs, three sheep, and four goats. The bunny died last year, but Jill just started feeding two stray cats. Being cheap, I tried to rationalize having all these animals by thinking that they could mow the grass. But one day as I was fixing a fence, I had a moment of profound enlightenment: "This is not saving us money. I am a zookeeper."

Several years ago when we had only three goats and one sheep, the weather forecasters predicted "the snowstorm of the century." They were calling for thirty inches of snow over the weekend. Jill was very concerned about the animals in their little wooden sheds. I called a sheep farmer and asked him if the animals would be okay. He assured me that as long they had a shelter they would be fine. I told Jill, and that seemed to help. (I was actually just trying to avoid having them in our bedroom.) As a precaution we put the goats in the garage, but our sheep, Ed, was still outside.

Saturday evening the snow was coming down heavily, and Jill got anxious. I reminded her of what the farmer had said, and she seemed okay. I had gone to bed and was dozing off when I heard Jill's voice in the dark, "Paul, I'm afraid for Ed. Would you check him?"

In my semiconscious state, I plotted my response. First, I'd appeal to the expert: the farmer. I'd quote him. Then, I'd resort to basic science and the insulating value of snow. But I knew science wouldn't change Jill's mind. So I decided to tell her she was obsessing over her animals. She'd then remind me that I had known that she loved animals before our marriage (in other words, she wasn't liable because of her product warning!). So, I'd first be cool and rational, and when that failed, I'd just flail her with words. But no matter what I said, she would go out and check Ed, and that would really make me mad.

I was left with making a choice of who got cold: either Jill went outside or I did. If I wanted to help Jill, I would have to exchange the warmth of my bed for the coldness of a winter storm. I had to sacrifice my warmth for her worry. I knew the issue wasn't whether the sheep was cold—the issue was Jill's anxiety. For five minutes of pain, I could give Jill eight hours of rest. So I got up, put on my clothes and boots, and checked on Ed.

Love Demands an Exchange

Every love story has an "exchange" in it. In *The Beauty and the Beast*, Belle redeems her father from the Beast by going in his place. Later, the Beast allows Belle to return home, giving up all hope of being loved by anyone. He gives up his joy for the sake of her happiness.

When Jesus lets the woman in Simon's house touch his feet, he took her bad reputation upon himself. At the same time, his acceptance of her repentance honored her. Jesus got her shame; she got his dignity. When Jesus invited himself over to Zacchaeus's house, the disdain that people felt for the tax collector came on Jesus.

The father in the parable about the Lost Son also takes on a burden when he runs to his returning son. Middle Eastern village patriarchs don't run, they walk with a stately stride. For this father,

LOVE WALKED AMONG US

running to his son is as shameful as wearing boxer shorts and a T-shirt to a formal dinner. The father runs because the whole village is so angry at his son for shaming them, that they will stone the son on the outskirts of the village. The father has to get to his son before the mob in order to protect him and to show the village how he wants him to be greeted. He "puts on boxer shorts" in order to spare his son from shame. He runs the gauntlet for him.[1]

An exchange occurs when we love. If Jill asks me to vacuum when I am watching the news, I substitute my free time for hers. If, at the office party, you seek out people who are lonely, whose personalities don't draw people, you exchange your enjoyment of the party for their happiness.

When James and John made their power play, Jesus said that he *did not come to be served, but to serve, and to give his life as a ransom for many (Mark 10:45)*. In ancient times, if your city was captured and you were enslaved, your friends could buy you back. They could substitute their money for your life. Jesus said that he will substitute his life for ours.

Up till now Jesus has been freeing trapped individuals: an outcast woman, a sick child, a disabled man—some from physical ailments, some from spiritual ailments. But it is a drop in the bucket, and there are millions of buckets—all leaking. Now Jesus claims that in his death he is going after the biggest need of all.

How is Jesus' death the center of all his love? What could Jesus possibly be exchanging?

The Ultimate Exchange of Love

Jesus' death occurred during the Passover holiday. For the original Passover in Egypt, each Israelite family killed a lamb and smeared its blood around their front doors so that they would be spared from death. The lamb took the place of the firstborn son who was about to die because of evil. Every spring, at the time of the barley harvest, the Israelites would reenact this meal. Americans do something similar when we reenact the Pilgrims' first Thanksgiving feast.

Jesus' last meal with the disciples was a Passover meal. After they had eaten the lamb, Jesus told the disciples that he is our Passover lamb: *Then he took the cup, gave thanks and offered it to them, saying, "Drink from it, all of you. This is my blood of the covenant, which is poured out for many for the forgiveness of sins"* (Matthew 26:27-28).

The forgiveness of sin through the shedding of blood was an idea deeply imbedded in the psyche of Israel and the whole ancient world. Every day the priests sacrificed hundreds of animals in the temple for the forgiveness of sins. The volume of the blood flowing out of the temple was so great that the stream outside the temple was called Kidron, or "black"—spilled blood turns black.

But the disciples didn't understand. Messiahs don't die for other people so they can be free; they make Romans die so that the Messiah and his followers can be free. But Jesus clearly tells them that his death is an act of love in which, like a Passover lamb, his blood will be *poured out for them.*

We might not understand either. We might say, "Back then people believed that evil was eradicated through the shedding of blood, but we don't believe it today." But how was the evil of Hitler and Nazism removed? Blood was shed. Millions lost their lives. Abraham Lincoln came to believe that a kind of exchange occurred on the battlefields of the Civil War, in which ". . . every drop of blood drawn with the lash shall be paid by another drawn with the sword."[2] Evil is not eradicated without a cost. You can't delete evil with the stroke of a key. It is far too embedded. It infects every part of the system.

Earlier Jesus told his disciples, *"I am the good shepherd . . . and I lay down my life for the sheep"* (John 10:14-15). The good shepherd became the lamb. Hundreds of years before, the prophet Isaiah had described a "suffering servant" who would substitute his life for the sheep: *"We all, like sheep, have gone astray, each of us has turned to his own*

LOVE WALKED AMONG US

way; and the LORD *has laid on him the iniquity of us all. . . . He was led like a lamb to the slaughter."* This "suffering servant" would be wounded and crushed for our sins . . . beaten that we might have peace. He was whipped, and we were healed (Isaiah 53:5-7). On the cross Jesus took our sin so that we could receive his goodness. He took our inability to love, our self-love, upon himself. He took our brokenness so that we could be healed.

Jesus said his death would be *for the forgiveness of sins.* Earlier he had told the woman in Simon's house, *"Your sins are forgiven";* a claim that he was the agent of God's forgiveness. But his forgiveness of the woman was like a post-dated check without money behind it until later. By dying, Jesus put money behind the check. By dying, he paid the cost of forgiveness. His death makes sense as the ultimate exchange of love to meet the deepest human need.

THE DEEPEST HUMAN NEED

The very nature of the need—forgiveness for sin—means that Jesus' death will be underappreciated. Most people don't think they have a problem. Simon the Pharisee certainly didn't. Why? Sin is pride—self-absorption, self-glorification, and even its flipside, self-loathing. Pride doesn't see itself as proud—that's its very nature. Jesus puts his finger on this in his story of the Pharisee and the Tax Collector. The Pharisee prays, *"God, I thank you that I am not like other men—robbers, evildoers, adulterers—or even like this tax collector"* (Luke 18:11).

While in a Russian prison camp, Aleksandr Solzhenitsyn was shaken by the depth of his hatred for his persecutors. He came to a new realization about himself:

> If only there were people somewhere committing evil deeds, and it were necessary only to separate them from the rest of us and destroy them. But the line dividing good

and evil cuts through the heart of every human being. Confronted with the pit into which we are about to toss those who have done us harm, we halt stricken dumb: it is after all only because of the way things worked out that they were the executioners and we weren't.[3]

He was able to say, "I have evil in me too." Evil isn't just out there. It's in us. As we've seen, Jesus repeatedly takes our pointing finger and gently turns it back toward us. He interrupts our quiet superiority and blame shifting by holding a mirror up to our faces. The problem isn't other people, it's me. It's me saying, "I am the boss. My will be done."

Because we have trouble seeing this, we also have trouble seeing that our evil has consequences. It just doesn't seem that bad. God's anger at sin seems like an overreaction. But Jesus sees both our sin and its consequences. He prayed in Gethsemane, *"Take this cup from me."* When Israel sinned, they *drank the cup of God's wrath.* If you drive drunk and kill someone, you *drink the cup* when you go to prison. If you use drugs, then you *drink the cup* when you get hepatitis. Sin always has consequences.

When we see something wrong, we don't ignore it. The rapist or child molester should go to jail, not just to protect society, but also to "pay for his crimes." He deserves it. We all deserve the cost of our sin.

On the cross, Jesus took what we deserve when he *drank the cup of God's wrath.* The payment for everything that we have done wrong was compressed into a few hours of agony on the cross. When we offend someone, we just don't offend the other person, we offend God. He is in community with us. Why would he be angry? Turn on the news—kids shooting guns in schools, politicians lying, nations fighting. Jesus' gift of love makes sense if we accept Jesus' assessment of us—we're empty people who need to be filled, selfish people who need to be turned outward, sinners who need to be forgiven. The more you see your sin, the

LOVE WALKED AMONG US

more you see the beauty of his sacrifice.

God can't just ignore our sin, because he's as committed to honesty and justice as he is to compassion. He's drawn to us, but he recoils from our evil. It's like trying to hug someone who is putting a knife in your back. You either have to stop hugging or get rid of the knife. God turns his justice on his Son so he can show us his mercy. Jesus takes the knife in order to embrace us in God's love. Jesus described himself as the barnyard hen whose body is seared by the fire, her life for her chicks. One life as a ransom for many.

But Jesus had never known the silence of his Father. What would it be like to be in the closest possible loving intimacy with someone for fifty years? One thousand years? From before time? Jesus has never been separated from his Father—until the cross. The thought of this alienation—so undeserved—horrifies Jesus. So on the cross, lost in a sea of human evil, separated from his all-loving Father, Jesus cries out, *"My God, my God, why have you forsaken me?"*

Why would Jesus endure separation from the Father? Some thirty years after Jesus' death and resurrection the writer of letter to the Hebrews wrote: *Fix [your] eyes on Jesus . . . who for the joy set before him endured the cross, scorning its shame, and sat down at the right hand of the throne of God (Hebrews 12:2).* Jesus knew that the coming joy was greater than the present sadness. The joy of being with the Father in an expanded circle of his love made the cost bearable.

ENJOYING THE GAZE OF GOD

Jesus' death offers an inner/soul healing—the same thing he gave to the woman at Simon's house and to Zacchaeus. A clean start. Past failures and sins forgiven and forgotten. It's God's stamp of love on us.

In *Harry Potter and the Sorcerer's Stone,* Harry learns why the villain, Voldemort, doesn't destroy him.

237

Your mother died to save you. If there is one thing Voldemort cannot understand, it is love. He didn't realize that love, as your mother's for you, leaves its own mark. Not a scar, no visible sign . . . to have been loved so deeply, even though the person who loved us is gone, will give us some protection forever. It is in your very skin.[4]

If you take Jesus' gift, it means that God doesn't just love you; he enjoys and delights in you. He wants you to be part of his life.

When Jill bought a donkey with her cleaning money, a friend of mine asked me, "What does your wife do with a donkey?" I knew he golfed, so I said, "The same thing you do with golf." Sometimes I'll see Jill resting on the fence, smiling, just looking at the donkey. I think it is the big, soft ears that get her. At least Jill told me that if I had big soft ears, she'd look at me the same way. When I see Jill enjoying her donkey, I get a glimpse into God's heart. Because of Jesus' death, God leans against the fence, looking at me, with a smile of pure delight on his face.

CHAPTER TWENTY-THREE

THE BIRTH OF HOPE

THE END OF
LOVE'S JOURNEY

*W*HILE READING AN ISSUE OF *MONEY* MAGAZINE devoted to retirement, I was struck that if an alien read this magazine, he'd assume that humans live forever; because it appeared that you could endlessly accumulate wealth. Jesus told a parable about a rich man who denied the reality of death and acted as if he would live forever. God told him, *"You fool! This very night your life will be demanded from you. Then who will get what you have prepared for yourself?"* (*Luke* 12:20). Death hangs over every life, every relationship.

When Jesus saw his friends Mary and Martha grieving over the death of their brother Lazarus, *he was deeply moved in spirit and troubled. "Where have you laid him?" he asked. "Come and see, Lord," they replied. Jesus wept* (*John* 11:33-35). *Deeply moved in spirit* is best translated as "outraged in spirit." He was steaming—like a boiling pot whose lid is about to blow off. His anger and agitation boiled over into a stream of tears. Jesus was angry at death and its effect on those he loves. Death is not part of the beauty of life; it is part of the brokenness that love seeks to mend.

Jesus didn't accept death as normal, and neither do we. Death may be commonplace, but it doesn't feel normal — it wasn't meant to be.

But Jesus didn't just weep over Lazarus. He wanted to know where the body was. The warrior-king was looking for the battle. His hand was on his sword. Earlier Martha (true to form!) had berated Jesus for being late, *"If you had been here, my brother would not have died." . . . Jesus responded, "I am the resurrection and the life. He who believes in me will live, even though he dies" (John 11:21,25)*. Jesus claimed he was not only the dying one, but also the living one.

But Jesus was swallowed up by the very thing he hated. The crucifixion had done its ugly work.

What's the point of love if the journey ends in despair? Love is what you do on the journey. Faith is how you make it through the journey. But hope is the end of journey. Without hope, love makes no sense.

THE BIRTH OF HOPE

The Sunday after Jesus' death, the disciples, petrified of the authorities, have locked themselves in the same upper room where they had their last meal with Jesus. But physical needs quietly demand attention. Some of the women who have followed Jesus visit the tomb before dawn to anoint Jesus' body with spices. They arrive to discover the stone moved and the guards gone. Entering the tomb, they find *a young man dressed in a white robe sitting on the right side.* He says to them, *"Why do you look for the living among the dead? He is not here; he has risen!" (Mark 16:5; Luke 24:5-6).*

Trembling and bewildered, the women went out and fled from the tomb (Mark 16:8) and reported to the disciples what they'd seen, *but they did not believe the women, because their words seemed to them like nonsense* (Luke 24:11). Dead men don't rise.

But Peter and John, followed by Mary Magdalene, sprint for the tomb. Once there, Peter sees *the strips of linen lying there . . . as well as the burial cloth that had been around Jesus' head. The cloth was folded up by itself, separate from the linen.* The men return home, *but Mary stood outside the tomb crying* (John 20:4-8,11).

Where's the body?

> [Mary] *turned around and saw Jesus standing there, but she did not realize that it was Jesus. "Woman," he said, "why are you crying? Who is it you are looking for?" Thinking he was the gardener, she said, "Sir, if you have carried him away, tell me where you have put him, and I will get him."*
>
> *Jesus said to her, "Mary." (John 20:14-16)*

Jesus' one-word response sounds just like him—so understated and tender. Hearing her name spoken by Jesus, Mary *turned toward him and cried out in Aramaic, "Rabboni!" (which means Teacher),* and she clings to Jesus. The last time she let him out of her sight, they took him away. She's not about to let it happen again. But Jesus has something better in mind: *"Do not hold on to me, for I have not yet returned to the Father. Go instead to my brothers and tell them, 'I am returning to my Father and your Father, to my God and your God'"* (20:17).

After Jesus goes to his Father, the Spirit will come, filling those who believe with the very person of Jesus, teaching them to love, to become like him. "His" Father becomes "your" Father. All who believe can now feel the closeness Jesus had with his Father. So Jesus tells his "sister" Mary to go tell his "brothers," the disciples, that everything is okay.

If the Father raised the Son, then everything is different. If death is conquered, then we have reason to love and give our life away. If Jesus is alive, then he can still surprise us. Hope is born.

In a world where a woman's testimony in court meant nothing, Jesus appears first to women. He never stops loving and honoring the weak and powerless. If you were trying to prove

241

the resurrection to a first-century audience, you'd never mention women as witnesses—unless it really happened that way.

The Same Person — A New Body

Later that day, two disciples leave Jerusalem and walk toward the town of Emmaus. *Jesus himself came up and walked along with them; but they were kept from recognizing him.* As he often does, Jesus begins with a question: *"What are you discussing together as you walk along?"* (Luke 24:15-17). They tell him about Jesus, a prophet whom they had thought would rescue Israel but who was killed by the rulers. Yet they are puzzled—just this morning women reported a vision of angels who said that Jesus was raised from death.

Jesus responds: *"How foolish you are, and how slow of heart to believe all that the prophets have spoken! Did not the Christ have to suffer these things and then enter his glory?"* (Luke 24:25-26). Can you hear his tone, the cadence of his words? He could easily be out on the Sea of Galilee again, scolding the disciples for worrying about bread. He doesn't miss a beat.

When they arrive at Emmaus, Jesus accepts their invitation to dinner, and as he breaks the bread, he disappears. They hurry back to Jerusalem, and during their report to the disciples, suddenly . . .

> *Jesus himself stood among them and said to them, "Peace be with you."*
>
> *They were startled and frightened, thinking they saw a ghost. He said to them, "Why are you troubled, and why do doubts rise in your minds? Look at my hands and my feet. It is I myself! Touch me and see; a ghost does not have flesh and bones, as you see I have."*
>
> *When he had said this, he showed them his hands and feet. And while they still did not believe it because of joy and amazement, he asked them, "Do you have anything here to eat?" They gave him a piece of broiled fish, and he took it and ate it in their presence.* (Luke 24:36-43)

LOVE WALKED AMONG US

The resurrected Jesus ate bread and had a body, a new body that could appear and disappear. His new, living body is the beginning of a completely new creation.

At the tomb the angel described Jesus as *the Living One*. Near the end of John's life, Jesus appears to John and uses the same description: *"Do not be afraid . . . I am the Living One; I was dead, and behold I am alive for ever and ever! And I hold the keys of death and Hades" (Revelation 1:17-18). The Living One* has swallowed up death. The seed that died is now reborn.

At the cross, Jesus broke the power of sin. At the resurrection, Jesus broke the power of death. Both need to be broken. If you solve only the problem of sin, then we'd all love one another, but death would haunt every relationship. If you solve only the problem of death, then we'd live forever in hatred.

The resurrection proved Jesus' claim that his death was for the forgiveness of sins. Peter, fifty days after Passover at the feast of Pentecost, told a crowd, *"God has made this Jesus, whom you crucified, both Lord and Christ" (Acts 2:36).* Jesus had said, "I forgive sins. My death is for the forgiveness of sins." The religious rulers said, "Only God can do that; therefore you should die because you're committing blasphemy." But God has the final word. By raising Jesus from the dead, the Father vindicated his Son and reversed their judgment: Jesus "can" forgive sins. Now his forgiveness is open to all of us. Since he's still alive, he can say to each of us, "Your sins are forgiven. The past is forgotten."

THE SCARS OF LOVE

But just ten disciples had seen Jesus—Judas was dead and Thomas was missing. Our few glimpses of Thomas suggest a realistic person, not prone to believe fantastic reports. When Jesus decided to go to Jerusalem in the face of death threats, Thomas *said to the rest of the disciples, "Let us also go, that we may die with him" (John 11:16).* Thomas courageously faces the facts but succumbs easily to pessimism.

At the Last Supper when Jesus used an allegory to talk about his departing, Thomas said, *"Lord, we don't know where you are going, so how can we know the way?"* (John 14:5) "Don't give me poetry, Jesus. Show me how this works." He is completely rooted to the earth. Thomas was likely never snookered, at least not twice. So when he hears the report of Jesus' resurrection he scoffs,

> *"Unless I see the nail marks in his hands and put my finger where the nails were, and put my hand into his side, I will not believe it."*
>
> *A week later, his disciples were in the house again, and Thomas was with them. Though the doors were locked, Jesus came and stood among them and said, "Peace be with you!"*
>
> *Then he said to Thomas, "Put your finger here; see my hands. Reach out your hand and put it into my side. Stop doubting and believe."*
>
> *Thomas said to him, "My Lord and my God!"*
>
> *Then Jesus told him, "Because you have seen me, you have believed; blessed are those who have not seen and yet have believed."*
> (John 20:25-29)

Jesus doesn't say, "Look how special I am because I resurrected." He says, "Look at my wounds. *Put your finger here; see my hands . . . and believe.*" Thomas sees and believes that God stands in front of him. A crucified God. The Pharisees finally get their sign—visible verification that Jesus is from God. Scars. The wounds of love. What a strange God, who doesn't remain aloof, but enters our world and becomes wounded.

Through his wounds, we can see him. Through the scar that God gave Kim, Jill and I have also learned to see Jesus. Our limp has been a severe mercy, making us dependent on God. Our scar speaks to us and tells us of the love of God. Our suffering with her has taught us to endure.

The hardest part of love is just hanging in there, continuing to

244

show up for life when the drama is over and we're locked in our upper room without plans or hope. But think of this: Jesus has a body. When Jesus became a person, he became a person forever. He didn't just hold his nose for thirty years, and then it was all over. He, the Son of God, was permanently changed because of his love for humanity. So if loving means changes for me, that is okay—it meant permanent change for Jesus. Love is forever.

AN INSIDE FRIEND

At the Last Supper Jesus promised his disciples that after his departure, "I will not leave you as orphans. I will come to you." He promised to send an *Encourager*—the Spirit who *"will take from what is mine and make it known to you"* (John 16:14-15). And after he shows the disciples his scars, Jesus fulfills his promise. He tells his disciples, *"As the Father has sent me, I am sending you." And with that he breathed on them and said, "Receive the Holy Spirit"* (John 20:21-22). Through the Spirit, we receive the very character of Jesus—his instincts, his heart, his boldness.

Jesus gives us a relationship, an inner guide to accompany us through the labyrinth of love. He spurs us on to love. Love, then, is not a hopeless, uphill task. With Jesus alive and "on the inside," the disciples begin to sound like their master, something that they had not been able to do before. When Peter and John are accosted by a crippled man outside the temple,

> *Peter looked straight at him, as did John. Then Peter said, "Look at us!" So the man gave them his attention, expecting to get something from them.*
>
> *Then Peter said, "Silver and gold I do not have, but what I have I give you. In the name of Jesus Christ of Nazareth, walk." Taking him by the right hand, he helped him up, and instantly the man's feet and ankles became strong. (Acts 3:4-7)*

245

They look, touch, then help. They finally get it!

Then the religious leaders interrogate Peter and John. To their horror, they recognize the dim outline of their old nemesis, Jesus. When the leaders *saw the courage of Peter and John and realized that they were unschooled, ordinary men, they were astonished and they took note that these men had been with Jesus (4:13).* Jesus' followers are beginning to look like Jesus; they have the same freedom from people's opinions, the same awareness of God.

The followers of Jesus, albeit haltingly, continue on the life of Jesus to this day. As Germany came under Hitler's sway, Einstein was struck by a strange life in the church:

> Having always been an ardent partisan of freedom, I turned to the universities, as soon as the revolution broke out in Germany, to find there the defenders of freedom. I did not find them. Very soon the universities took refuge in silence.
>
> I then turned to the editors of powerful newspapers who, but lately in flowing articles, had claimed to be the faithful champions of liberty. These men, as well as the universities, were reduced to silence within a few weeks.
>
> I then addressed myself to the authors individually, to those who passed themselves off as the intellectual guides of Germany, and among whom many had frequently discussed the question of freedom and its place in modern life. They were in their turn silent.
>
> Only the Church opposed the fight which Hitler was waging against liberty. Till then I had no interest in the Church, but now I feel a great admiration and am truly attracted to the Church which had the persistent courage to fight for spiritual truth and moral freedom.
>
> I feel obliged to confess that I now admire what I used to consider of little value.[1]

LOVE WALKED AMONG US

Jesus was with lowly people in his life on earth so, not surprisingly, he is there now. Mother Teresa relates this encounter with an old man in Calcutta ("old man" is a term of respect):

"Who is this Christ of Mother Teresa's?"

"He's our Guru, old man, our Lord and our God."

"What God is this?"

"He's a God of love, old man. He loves all of us—me and you too!"

"How could he love me, Mem Sahib? He doesn't even know me."

"Oh yes he does! Didn't he reach right out across the city for you? Did he send his Sisters to the slums of Motijhil to bring you here? Doesn't he love you then, old man?"

After a pause the old man said: "Could I love him, do you think?"

"Of course you could—it's easy to love him—we'll love him together old man, but sleep now. We'll talk again in the morning. Sleep now old man."[2]

Mother Teresa said of her work with the poor: "We are doing it with Jesus, for Jesus, to Jesus."[3] To care for the weak is to love Jesus. Jesus said: *"For I was hungry and you gave me something to eat, I was thirsty and you gave me something to drink, I was a stranger and you invited me in, I needed clothes and you clothed me, I was sick and you looked after me, I was in prison and you came to visit me"* (Matthew 25:35-36).

Mother Teresa and others like her who love in the name of Jesus are often seen as great humanitarians. They are not. When an interviewer complimented Mother Teresa that she can "pick up a telephone and reach a President and a Prime Minister because you speak in the name of peace," Mother Teresa replied, "In the name of Christ. Without him I could do nothing."[4]

He Loves to Love

When Jesus left this earth to return to heaven to be with his Father, he promised that he would come again. He likened his return to a groom coming for his bride. At the wedding feast where he welcomes his bride, his followers, Jesus describes what he will do: "*. . . he will dress himself to serve, will have them recline at the table and will come and wait on them*" (*Luke* 12:37).

Jesus wants to serve at his own wedding—set the table, replenish our drinks, and show us the dessert tray. Jesus is nothing if not consistent. Even at the end, he is drawn to the low place. He loves to love.

Chapter Twenty-Four

OPENING THE DOOR

What Do We Do with Jesus?

C. S. Lewis asks:

"What are we to make of Christ?" There is no question of what we can make of him, it is entirely a question of what he intends to make of us. You must accept or reject the story.

The things he says are very different from what any other teacher has said. Others say, "This is the truth about the Universe. This is the way you ought to go," but he says, "I am the truth, and the way, and the life." He says, "No man can reach absolute reality, except through me. Try to retain your own life and you will be inevitably ruined. Give yourself away and you will be saved." He says, "If you are ashamed of me, if, when you hear this call, you turn the other way, I also will look the other way when I come again as God without disguise. If anything whatever is keeping you from God and from me, whatever it is, throw it away. If it is your eye, pull it out. If it is your hand, cut it off. If you put yourself first, you will be last. Come to me everyone who is carrying a heavy load, I will set that right. Your sins, all of them, are wiped out, I can do that. I am Re-birth, I am Life. Eat Me, drink Me, I am your Food. And finally, do not be afraid, I have overcome the whole Universe." That is the issue.[1]

If Jesus is alive, then we can push our way through the crowd, like the bleeding woman, and silently touch his garment. But he won't let us quietly slip away in the crowd. He'll call to us as he did Anne Lamott, a best-selling author.

It's not about the experience but it's about the Word of God. the experience can leads us to the Word.

> I didn't go to the flea market the week of my abortion. I stayed home, and smoked dope and got drunk, and tried to write a little. . . . On the seventh night, though very drunk . . . I discovered that I was bleeding heavily. . . . I thought I should call a doctor . . . but I was so disgusted that I had gotten so drunk one week after an abortion that I just couldn't wake someone up and ask for help . . . I got in bed, shaky and sad and too wild to have another drink or take a sleeping pill. I had a cigarette and turned off the light. After a while, as I lay there, I became aware of someone with me, hunkered down in the corner. . . . The feeling was so strong that I actually turned on a light for a moment to make sure no one was there—of course, there wasn't. But after a while, in the dark again, I knew beyond doubt that it was Jesus. I felt him as surely as I feel my dog lying nearby as I write this.
>
> And I was appalled. I thought about my life and my brilliant hilarious progressive friends, I thought about what everyone would think of me if I became a Christian, and it seemed an utterly impossible thing that simply could not be allowed to happen. I turned to the wall and said out loud, "I would rather die."

LOVE WALKED AMONG US

I felt him just sitting there on his haunches in the corner of my sleeping loft, watching me with patience and love, and I squinched my eyes shut, but that didn't help because that's not what I was seeing him with.

Finally I fell asleep, and in the morning, he was gone.

This experience spooked me badly, but I thought it was just an apparition, born of fear and self-loathing and booze and loss of blood. But then everywhere I went, I had the feeling that a little cat was following me, wanting me to reach down and pick it up, wanting me to open the door and let it in. But I knew what would happen: you let a cat in one time, give it a little milk, and then it stays forever. So I tried to keep one step ahead of it, slamming my houseboat door when I entered or left.

And one week later, when I went back to church, I was so hung over that I couldn't stand up for the songs, and this time I stayed for the sermon, which I just thought was so ridiculous, like someone trying to convince me of the existence of extraterrestrials, but the last song was so deep and raw and pure that I could not escape. It was as if the people were singing in between the notes, weeping and joyful at the same time, and I felt like their voices or *something* was rocking me in its bosom, holding me like a scared kid, and I opened up to that feeling—and it washed over me.

I began to cry . . . and I raced home and felt the little cat running along at my heels, and I walked down the dock past dozens of potted flowers, under a sky as blue as one of God's own dreams, and I opened the door to my houseboat, and I stood there a minute, and then I hung my head and said: ". . . I quit." I took a long deep breath and said out loud, "All right. You can come in."[2]

OPENING THE DOOR

Jesus intruded into Zacchaeus's life, into Anne Lamott's life, and he can intrude into your life. He touched lepers and healed them. He can touch the leprous parts of your life. He healed the sick. He can heal your lusts. He reached out his strong carpenter hands and invited little children up onto his lap. He invites you as well. He is the shepherd-king, someone both good and strong, who finds you in your deepest fears and meets your smallest needs. Like the father in the parable about the Lost Son, he is waiting, scanning the horizon.

And Jesus is still honest. When you are "doing your own thing," he turns and looks at you, like he did with Peter at the trial and with Anne Lamott in her room. His eyes see all. He invites you to come down to the low place, the place of seeing clearly.

When you invite Jesus in, he has a way of taking over the whole house. He's the king. He's gentle and understanding, but he wants nothing less than unconditional surrender. Kings don't say, "I'd like to have your vote." They say, "Come follow me." You don't say "no" when the king is calling. Jesus said that to hear his words and obey them is like a wise person who builds his house on solid rock. When the storms of life come, it stands firm. But the person who doesn't listen to his words is like a foolish person who builds his house on sand. When the storms of life come, it is blown away (Matthew 7:24-27). And storms will come.

Matthew was working in his tax office when Jesus passed by and said, *"Follow me" (Matthew 9:9)*. Matthew got up and left his office, never to return. Jesus is passing by now, saying, "Come, follow me." We can say with Blind Bartimaeus, *"Jesus, Son of David, have mercy on me."* Or we can walk away like the young wealthy man who was unable to follow Jesus because of the hold money had on him. If you find your inner voices telling you to "hush up" as the people did to Bartimaeus, you can shout all the louder, "JESUS, SON OF DAVID, HAVE MERCY ON ME!"

LOVE WALKED AMONG US

In the parable about the Lost Son, Jesus tells us what to say when we come home to God. Along with the lost son, you could say to your heavenly Father, "I've lived in your world but ignored you. I've done what felt good and it hasn't worked. I've not loved the way Jesus loved. I often put up a good front, yet there are those secret moments of despair that I tell no one about. I am empty. So now I come home asking your forgiveness. I lay my life down in your strong arms. I surrender. Thank you for welcoming me home."

Love didn't just walk among us. He can indwell us. Jesus repeatedly told people, "In me you'll find your deepest needs met—your need for forgiveness, love, hope, belonging, and purpose. I am what you've always been looking for."

INTRODUCTION

1. Jaroslav Pelikan, *Jesus Through the Centuries: His Place in the History of Culture* (New Haven: Yale University Press, 1985), p. 1.
2. George Viereck, "What Life Means to Einstein," *Saturday Evening Post* (Oct. 26, 1929): p. 117.
3. Viereck, p. 117.
4. C. S. Lewis, *God in the Dock* (Grand Rapids, MI: Eerdmans, 1994), p. 158.

CHAPTER 1

1. Alfred Edersheim, *Sketches of Jewish Social Life: Updated Edition* (Peabody, MA: 1994), p. 153.
2. Alfred Edersheim, *The Life and Times of Jesus the Messiah*, vol. 1 (Grand Rapids, MI: Eerdmans, 1971), pp. 552-559.
3. Arnold Dallimore, *Spurgeon: A New Biography* (Edinburgh: Banner of Truth Trust, 1985), p. 58.
4. Dallimore, p. 58.

CHAPTER 2

1. Kenneth Bailey, *Poet and Peasant* (Grand Rapids, MI: Eerdmans, 1976), p. 164.

2. Navin Chawla, *Mother Teresa* (Rockport, Mass: Element Books, 1996), p. 203.
3. Kenneth Bailey, *Through Peasant Eyes* (Grand Rapids, MI: Eerdmans, 1980), p. 52.
4. Jonathan Coleman, "Is Technology Making Us Intimate Strangers?" *Newsweek* (March 27, 2000): p. 12.
5. Corrie ten Boom with Carole C. Carlson, *In My Father's House,* (Old Tappan, NJ: Fleming Revell, 1976), pp. 82-84.

CHAPTER 3
1. D. A. Carson, *The Gospel According to John* (Grand Rapids, MI: InterVarsity, 1991), p. 373.
2. Henri J. M. Nouwen, *The Way of the Heart* (San Francisco: Harper, 1991), p. 35.

CHAPTER 4
1. Kenneth E. Bailey, *Through Peasant Eyes* (Grand Rapids, MI: Eerdmans, 1980), p. 8.
2. Bailey, p. 8.
3. My dad, Jack Miller, used to say, "Cheer up, you're much worse than you think!"

CHAPTER 5
1. Sigmund Freud and Oskar Pfister, *Psychoanalysis and Faith: The Letters of Sigmund Freud and Oskar Pfister,* trans. E. Mosbacher, ed. H. Men and E. L. Freud (New York: Basic, 1963), p. 61.
2. D. A. Carson, Douglas J. Moo, and Leon Morris, *An Introduction to the Old Testament* (Grand Rapids, MI: Zondervan, 1992), p.129.
3. Jean-Paul Sartre, *Being and Nothingness,* trans. Hazel E. Barnes (New York: Philosophical Library, 1956), p. 260.

NOTES

CHAPTER 8

1. Robertson McQuilkin, "Muriel's Blessing," *Christianity Today*,
   (Feb 5, 1996): p. 33.
2. Alfred Edersheim, *The Life and Times of Jesus the Messiah*, vol. 1
   (Grand Rapids, MI: Eerdmans, 1971), p. 435.
3. Composite of Luke 6:6-7; Matthew 12:10-12; Mark 3:3-6.
4. Alfred Edersheim, *The Life and Times of Jesus the Messiah*, vol. 2
   (Grand Rapids, MI: Eerdmans, 1971), p. 377.
5. C. S. Lewis, *The Lion, the Witch, and the Wardrobe* (New York:
   Macmillan, 1950), pp. 75-76.
6. Fydor Dostoevsky, *The Brothers Karamazov* (New York:
   Bantam Books, 1970), p. 708.

CHAPTER 9

1. N. T. Wright, *Jesus and the Victory of God* (Minneapolis, MN:
   Fortress Press, 1996), p. 290.

CHAPTER 10

1. I substituted "beam" for "plank."
2. D. A. Carson, *The Gospel According to John* (Downers Grove,
   IL: InterVarsity, 1991), p. 336; Raymond Brown, *The Gospel
   According to John*, vol. I (New York: Doubleday, 1966), p. 337.
3. N. T. Wright, *Jesus and the Victory of God* (Minneapolis, MN:
   Fortress Press, 1996), p. 397.

CHAPTER 11

1. Robert McQuilkin, "Muriel's Blessing," *Christianity Today*
   (Feb. 5, 1996): pp. 33-34.
2. George Viereck, "What Life Means to Einstein," *Saturday
   Evening Post* (Oct. 26, 1929): p. 117.

CHAPTER 12

1. David M. May, "Mark 3:20-35 From the Perspective of Shame/ Honor." *Biblical Theological Bulletin* 17 (July 1987): pp. 83-87.
2. N. T. Wright, *Jesus and the Victory of God* (Minneaopolis, MN: Fortress Press, 1996), p. 453.

CHAPTER 13

1. Matthew 5:37; 6:13; 9:4; 12:34; Luke 6:45; 11:13; John 17:15.
2. My translation "since" for "if" from the Greek.
3. Margaret Alter, *Resurrection Psychology* (Chicago: Loyola University Press, 1994), p. 48.
4. Rabbi Eliezer, when his teaching was challenged, appealed to signs. He commanded a locust tree to move and made channels of water flow backward. (Talmudic Tractate Babba Metsia 59b, line 4 from top.)
5. Robertson McQuilkin, "Muriel's Blessing," *Christianity Today* (Feb. 5, 1996): p. 33.
6. Robertson McQuilkin, "Living by Vows," *Christianity Today* (Oct. 1990): pp. 38-40.
7. McQuilkin, "Muriel's Blessing," p. 33.
8. B. B. Warfield, *The Person and Work of Christ* (Philadelphia: Presbyterian & Reformed Publishing, 1950), p. 208.

CHAPTER 14

1. Anita Mathias, "The Holy Ground of Kalighat," *The Best Spiritual Writing 1999*, ed. Philip Zaleski (New York: HarperCollins, 1999), p. 192.

CHAPTER 15

1. "There had spread over all the Orient an old and established belief, that it was fated at that time for men coming from Judea to rule the world." Suetonius II, *The Lives of the Caesars*,

Book VIII, ed. G.P. Goold (Cambridge: Harvard University
Press, 1914), p. 289.

2. N. T. Wright, *The New Testament and the People of God*
(Minneapolis: Fortress Press, 1992), p. 176.

CHAPTER 16

1. In Hebrew *son of* includes the idea of "belonging to." So *Son
of God* had a potentially broad range of meanings including
"Israelite," a Davidic king, or a holy person.
2. C. S. Lewis, *The Silver Chair* (New York: Macmillan, 1953),
pp. 16-17.

CHAPTER 17

1. Likely the present-day Arab village of Askar.
2. Raymond Brown, *The Gospel According to John I-XII* (NewYork:
Doubleday, 1966), p. 173.
3. My translation from the Greek, *"What are you seeking?"*
4. Napoleon Bonaparte, "Conversations with General Bertrand
at St. Helena," Anthology of Jesus, arr. and sel. Sir James
Marchant, ed. Warren W. Werste (Grand Rapids: Kregel
Publications, 1981), p. 260.

CHAPTER 18

1. John is written in Greek, but his word meanings are distinc-
tively Hebrew.
2. Jean-Paul Sartre, *Being and Nothingness* (New York: Pocket
Books, 1984), p. 478.
3. Kenneth Bailey, *Poet and Peasant* (Grand Rapids, MI:
Eerdmans, 1976), p. 165.
4. D. M. Baille, *God Was in Christ: An Essay on Incarnation and
Atonement* (New York: Scribner's, 1948), pp. 205-206.

259

5. N. T. Wright, *Jesus and the Victory of God* (Minneapolis: Fortress Press, 1996), p. 433.

6. Bailey, p. 186.

CHAPTER 19

1. Henri J. M. Nouwen, *In the Name of Jesus* (New York: Crossroad, 1989), pp. 10-11.

2. "Beneath an octagonal fifth-century Byzantium church and a fourth century Jewish-Christian house synagogue, the remains of a private house were uncovered. It had, as early as the second half of the first century, served as an assembly hall for religious meetings. Inscriptions and the reports of early Christian travelers make it possible to identify the building as Peter's house." Ranier Riesner, "Archeology and Geography," *Dictionary of Jesus and the Disciples,* ed. Joel Green, Scot McKnight, and I. Howard Marshall (Downers Grove, IL: InterVarsity, 1992), p. 39.

3. Nouwen, p. 59.

4. Navin Chawla, *Mother Teresa* (Rockport, MA: Element Books, 1996), p. 205.

CHAPTER 20

1. C. S. Lewis, *The Four Loves* (New York: Harcourt Brace & Company, 1988), p. 121.

2. N. T. Wright, *Jesus and the Victory of God* (Minneapolis: Fortress Press, 1996), p. 587.

3. Wright, p. 333.

4. Thomas Cahill, *Desire of the Everlasting Hills* (New York: Doubleday, 1999), pp. 60-61.

CHAPTER 21

1. We know from Philo and Josephus, both contemporaries of Jesus, that Pilate hated the Jews. Harold W. Hoehner,

"Pilate," *Dictionary of Jesus and the Gospels* (Downers Grove, IL: InterVarsity, 1992), p. 615.

2. Crucifixion was so gruesome that the church did not use the cross as a symbol for over 350 years (well after crucifixion ceased to be used).

CHAPTER 22

1. Kenneth Bailey, *Poet and Peasant* (Grand Rapids, MI: Eerdmans, 1976), p. 180.

2. Abraham Lincoln, "Second Inaugural Address," in *Abraham Lincoln* by Carl Sandburg (New York: Harcourt, Brace, and Co., 1967), p. 664.

3. Aleksandr Solzhenitsyn, *The Gulag Archipelago: 1918-1965. An Experiment in Literary Investigation* (London: Book Club Associates, 1974), p.168.

4. J. K. Rowling, *Harry Potter and the Sorcerer's Stone* (New York: Scholastic Press, 1997), p. 299.

CHAPTER 23

1. Julius Rieger, *The Silent Church: The Problem of the German Confessional Witness* (London: S.C.M. Press Limited, 1944), p. 90.

2. Mother Teresa, *In the Silence of the Heart: Meditations by Mother Teresa of Calcutta* (London: SPCK, 1983), p. 43.

3. Navin Chawla, *Mother Teresa* (Rockport, MA: Element Books, 1996), p. 208.

4. Chawla, p. 202.

CHAPTER 24

1. C. S. Lewis, *God in the Dock*, ed. Walter Hooper (Grand Rapids, MI: Eerdmans, 1994), p. 160.

2. Anne Lamott, *Traveling Mercies* (New York: Pantheon Books, 1999), pp. 49-50.

ABOUT THE AUTHOR

AUL MILLER IS DIRECTOR OF *SEEJESUS*, which develops interactive Bible study guides that allow you to discover truths on your own within a small group. He is the author of *A Praying Life* and *The Person of Jesus, A Study of Love* on which this book is based. Like the book, it is written to teach people about how Jesus loves. He also teaches seminars that train people to lead the study with friends and neighbors. Paul and his wife, Jill, have six children, two sons-in-law, four goats, three sheep, two dogs, and a stray cat that Jill has just started feeding. They live near Philadelphia.

f you have questions or comments about Jesus or you are interested in using the study on which this book is based (*The Person of Jesus: A Study of Love*), I'd enjoy hearing from you. Contact me by any of the following ways: by e-mail at paulmiller@seeJesus.net, by our Web site at www.seeJesus.net, or drop me a note at P.O. Box 197, Telford, PA 18969.

Paul Miller

THERE'S MORE!

Now it's simple to teach what you've learned from *LOVE WALKED AMONG US.*

The Person of Jesus study is the perfect tool for leading your group. It goes much deeper than *Love Walked Among Us*, and its interactive format encourages discussion through thoughtful, exploratory questions.

People have taught *The Person of Jesus* study in all kinds of settings: • neighborhood studies • reading clubs • youth groups • coffee houses • prisons • restaurants • women's shelters • college campuses

Its simple approach makes it easy for anyone to teach!

❀

Get your **FREE** sample lesson by emailing info@seeJesus.net, calling toll-free 866-JesusNet (866-537-8763), or downloading from www.seeJesus.net.